THE COLOR BOOK OF
Beaded Jewelry

GENEVIEVE STERBENZ

PHOTOGRAPHY
Damian Sandone and Steven Mays

SENIOR EDITOR Carol Endler Sterbenz
PHOTO EDITOR Robyn Poplasky
EDITORIAL ASSISTANTS Jennifer Calvert and Nora Grace
INDEXER Schroeder Indexing Services
PRINCIPAL PHOTOGRAPHY Damian Sandone
INSTRUCTIONAL PHOTOGRAPHY Steven Mays
PRODUCER OF PHOTOGRAPHY Genevieve A. Sterbenz
STYLIST Robin del Pino
TECHNICAL EDITOR Candie Frankel
DESIGNER Goodesign

Creative Homeowner
VICE PRESIDENT AND PUBLISHER Timothy O. Bakke
PRODUCTION DIRECTOR Kimberly H. Vivas
ART DIRECTOR David Geer
MANAGING EDITOR Fran J. Donegan

ISBN-10: 1-58011-348-6
ISBN-13: 978-1-58011-348-9

Creative Homeowner®
A Division of Federal Marketing Corp.
24 Park Way
Upper Saddle River, NJ
www.creativehomeowner.com

*For my aunt, Shirley Smith,
whom I love and admire
for her strength, enthusiasm, and
joie de vivre.*

Introduction

THE COLOR BOOK OF BEADED JEWELRY IS A GORGEOUS COLLECTION OF 35 ORIGINAL PIECES OF JEWELRY MADE USING THE VAST ARRAY OF COLORFUL BEADS AVAILABLE TODAY. THE BOOK PRESENTS A DIVERSE ASSORTMENT OF BEAUTIFUL NECKLACES, BRACELETS, AND EARRINGS THAT ARE SURE TO DELIGHT, INSPIRE, AND CHALLENGE THE BEADING ENTHUSIAST. THIS UNIQUE VOLUME USES COLOR TO CATEGORIZE AND ORGANIZE THE JEWELRY WHILE EXPLAINING THE FUNDAMENTALS OF COLOR THEORY IN AN EFFORT TO INSTILL CONFIDENCE AND EXPAND THE CREATIVE POTENTIAL OF THE CRAFTER WHO WANTS TO DESIGN PIECES THAT CATER TO HER OWN PERSONAL SENSE OF TASTE AND STYLE.

Each chapter of the book is dedicated to an individual color of the rainbow, and one chapter is devoted to the always-in-style black and white. In the first chapter, red plays a starring role, boasting pieces of jewelry in both single shades and mixes of red. "China Rose" is a single-strand necklace made with hand-painted beads in Chinese red. "Candy Apple" is a nine-strand bracelet made in sparkling rough-cut "red delicious" beads, and "Sweetheart" is a multistrand necklace using bold combinations of beads in red and hot pink. Predictably, the **Red** chapter is followed by Orange and Yellow, Green, and so on, but this is where the "predictability" of **The Color Book of Beaded Jewelry** ends.

Each piece of jewelry is photographed in rich, exquisite detail, with swaths of sheer fabric providing colorful backdrops to the jewelry, inspiring an even broader set of choices for accent colors or completely new color combinations and design possibilities. Easy-to-follow directions guide the reader though each step in the jewelry-making process, **The Color Book of Beaded Jewelry** includes a "Beading Basics" section that introduces the essential tools, findings, stringing materials, and essential techniques to make each piece of jewelry featured in the book. Finally, a "Sources and Resources" section provides a handy listing of the places to buy the best in jewelry-making materials and supplies, rounding out this inspirational and practical guide to creating colorful and stunning masterpieces.

Table of Contents

Color Basics: Designing with Color

WE ALL HAVE FAVORITE COLORS—COLORS WE RESPOND TO, COLORS THAT AROUSE OUR SENSES, COLORS THAT STIMULATE AND INSPIRE OUR IMAGINATION. SOME COLORS ACTUALLY HELP EVOKE FEELINGS AND CONJURE MOODS, AS EVIDENCED BY COMMON IDIOMS AND EXPRESSIONS SUCH AS "SEEING RED," "TICKLED PINK," "GREEN WITH ENVY," AND "FEELING BLUE." WE DECORATE OUR LIVING SPACES IN COLORS THAT CALM OR EXCITE US. WE CHOOSE MAKEUP AND CLOTHING IN COLORS THAT FLATTER US OR SHOW US IN OUR BEST LIGHT. OUR SENSE OF COLOR GUIDES OUR DESIGN AND STYLE CHOICES AND OUR TASTE IN ATTIRE, AND IT STRONGLY INFLUENCES THE BEADS WE CHOOSE TO DESIGN OUR OWN JEWELRY. AFTER ALL, ONE OF THE MOST IMPORTANT PRINCIPLES OF DESIGN IS COLOR.

Browse through any bead store, and you will find rows of semiprecious stones arranged in blocks of color. Beaded strands of **red** coral, orange quartz, yellow citrine, green jade, **blue** turquoise, and **violet** amethyst create a rainbow of sparkling stones. But which beads to choose? And what is the best way to combine them?

The color wheel featured on the opposite page identifies the visible spectrum of colors and the relationships between them. **Red**, yellow, and **blue** are, of course, the three primary colors. Orange, green, and **violet** are secondary colors and the result of combining primary colors. Tertiary colors like **red**-orange, yellow-green, and **blue**-**violet** are created by combining a primary and a secondary color. Mix these colors with black, which is actually defined as the absence of light, or with white, which is the combination of all colors, and they will produce infinite numbers of tints and shades. Because black, white, and gray lack chromatic content, they are known as achromatic colors. Neutral colors are created when pure colors are combined with either white or black, or when two complementary colors are mixed together. These include browns, tans, pastels, and darker colors.

Familiarizing yourself with the color wheel will instill confidence when choosing color combinations for your jewelry designs. A monochromatic color scheme is one in which a single color or different shades of the same color are used, for instance light, medium, and dark **blue**. Analogous colors always look good together. These are related colors that sit next to one another on the color wheel—like the warm shades of **red**, orange, and yellow or the cool shades that range from green-**blue** to **blue**-**violet**. Warm colors are known to arouse and stimulate the senses while cool colors are known to achieve a calm, relaxing effect. Complementary colors sit opposite one another on the color wheel and share no common colors. Examples of these are **red** and green or yellow and **violet**. When combined, complementary colors can create bold contrast in beaded jewelry designs.

The science of color can be fascinating but the most important element of jewelry design is choosing colors that you love and can relate to. If you are going to take the time and effort to create an elegant bracelet to accent your favorite summer skirt or a necklace to offset a vibrant red jacket, select beads that speak to you in colors that you love to wear. If you choose beads in colors that inspire or move you, your sense of design will always reflect it, and you will find yourself making those signature pieces your favorites.

21

25

29

47

51

55

47

51

55

73

77

81

99

103

107

125

129

133

159

Red

Bold and daring, red is the color of passion and love—imagine a single-stem, burgundy-red rose, a lacy negligee in scarlet, or a cherry-red, heart-shaped box of chocolates. Diamonds may be forever, but they can't match the smoldering glow of a ruby or the inner fire of garnet for true romance. Red is also the color of power—slick on some fire-engine-red lipstick and you'll see why. There's a reason that VIPs walk the red carpet, and that ruby slippers changed the Wicked Witch: red packs a punch. Red packs its own heat, too. Think of the warm orange-red of a sun-ripened tomato or a field ablaze with poppies. But as hot as red can be, it can also chill out when mixed with blue—picture the color of ripe raspberries or a jewel-like glass of merlot. Red can also shift to hot pink, flamingo, magenta, or fuchsia. Add a touch of white, and red hues shift and soften to ballet pink and dusty rose. Red mixes beautifully with other warm-toned colors, like yellow and orange, producing warm amber and coral, for a blazing sunset feel. Or combine red with pink (like pink opal or rose quartz) for a sweetly sexy Valentine's look. Pairing cherry red with turquoise or aquamarine makes the colors "pop," like a 50s-era diner, while matching cinnabar red with deep-purple amethyst makes a strong, regal statement. Berry reds and forest greens, with a touch of metallic gold for sparkle, create holiday magic.

China Rose

Evoking the wonder and mystery of the Far East, this exotic necklace is composed of glass beads in fiery Chinese red. The ornate beads are adorned with hand-painted flowers and positioned in the central part of the necklace, while lengths of smaller, faceted coral beads extend from each side of the strand. Gold findings set with sparkling rhinestones and a gold clasp complete elegant "China Rose."

materials

- 9 round painted-glass beads, red with pink roses, 22mm dia.
- 48 faceted, round dyed-coral beads, red, 8mm dia.
- 4 round spacer beads, gold with red rhinestones, 6mm dia.
- 2 clamshells, gold
- 2 crimp tubes, gold, size 2
- 1 spring ring, gold, 18mm dia.
- 1 end ring in "figure-8" shape, gold
- Beading wire, 0.4mm dia.

tools

- Ruler, wire cutters, crimping pliers, 2 chain-nose pliers

techniques

- How to Use a Crimp Tube/Bead (See pg. 166.)
- How to Use a Clamshell (See pg. 167.)
- How to Use a Clamshell to Cover a Crimp Tube/Bead (See page 167.)
- How to Attach a Clamshell (See pg. 167.)

Finished length: 24" (60.9cm)

13

China Rose

1.

Use wire cutters to cut a 35-in. (88.9cm) length of beading wire. Attach one end of the beading wire to the spring ring using a crimp tube and the crimping pliers. Then cover the crimp tube with a clamshell.

2.

Use chain-nose pliers to attach the clamshell to the spring ring.

3.

String one spacer bead and one coral bead onto the beading wire, hiding the cut end of the wire in the beads.

4.

String on 23 more coral beads followed by one spacer bead, nine painted beads, another spacer bead, 24 coral beads, and the remaining spacer bead.

5.

Use crimping pliers, a crimp tube, and a clamshell to attach the "figure 8" ring to the end of the beading wire. Tuck the cut end of the beading wire into the last bead, trimming away any excess wire.

HELPFUL TIP

For a simpler design, use only the large painted-glass beads. Or, if the same bead is available in different sizes, combine them to create a symmetrical design with graduating-size beads. Position the smallest beads at the ends near the clasp and the largest beads in the center.

Candy Apple

Nine strands of beads, one totally captivating bracelet. For the red, delicious "Candy Apple," nine slender and separate strands of sparkling faceted beads are organized on a bar clasp to create a bracelet that is wide and substantial. The decorative sterling-silver clasp adds an accent of grace and refinement. The individual strands are strung with beads made of rough-cut glass, their uneven surfaces perfect for reflecting light in a glow of candy-apple red. The effect gives this fun and flashy bracelet a lush, opulent look.

materials

- 5 strands of rough, faceted round glass beads, red, 5mm dia. (Note: A 12" (30.5cm) strand is composed of approx. 90 beads.)
- 18 crimp tubes, silver, size 2
- Bar clasp for 5 strands, sterling silver
- Beading wire, 0.32mm dia.

tools

- Ruler
- Wire cutters
- Crimping pliers
- 2 chain-nose pliers

techniques

- How to Use a Crimp Tube/Bead (See pg. 166.)

Candy Apple

QUICK TIP

Using only one strand in the center hole of the bar clasp gives the beads space to move and allows them to lay flat when the bracelet is worn.

instructions

1.

Use wire cutters to cut nine 12-in. (30.4cm) lengths of beading wire. Attach one strand of beading wire to an outside hole on half of the clasp using a crimp tube and crimping pliers.

2.

Thread on 50 beads. This beaded wire should measure 7 in. (17.8cm).

3.

Use a crimp tube and the crimping pliers to attach the other end of the strand to the corresponding outside hole in the second half of the clasp. Tuck the wire end into the last beads.

4.

Repeat steps 1-3 to attach the remaining eight strands of beads. Attach two strands per hole with the exception of the center hole. Be sure to attach each strand end to the correct corresponding hole.

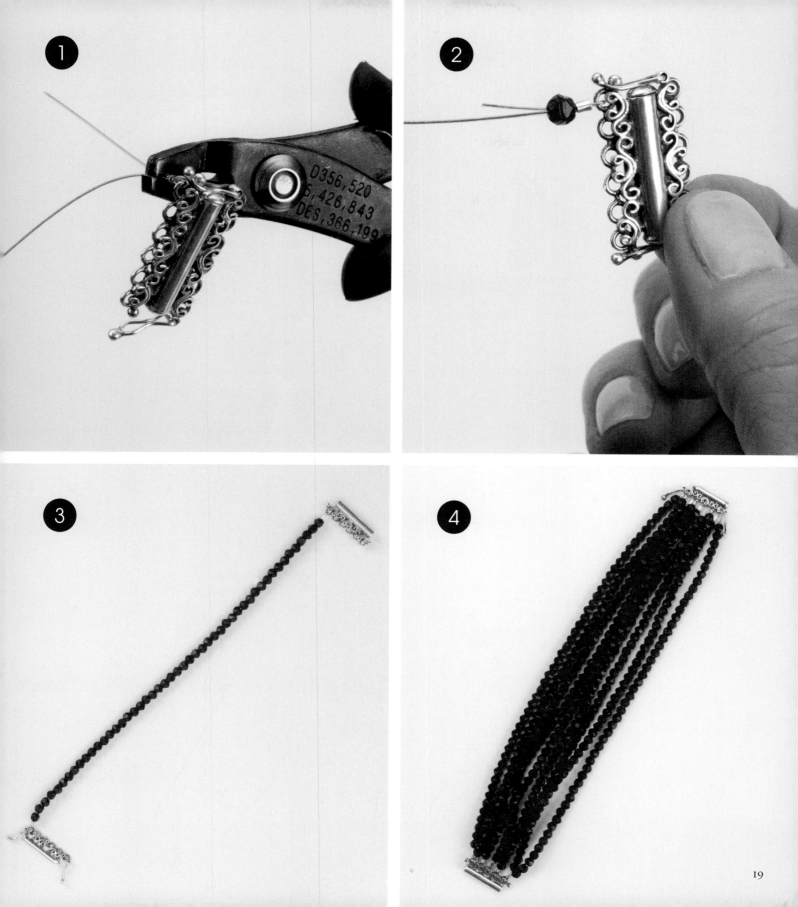

Fire and Ice

Who says fire and ice don't mix? A sexy combination of both hot and cool, these delicate Austrian-crystal earrings boast clear-as-water cubes that mimic the look of ice. The faceted cubes are buttressed by spacer beads, that are adorned with sparkling rhinestones the color of wine. Eye-pleasing bicone crystals in dazzling ruby red add flair and drama and are accented by tasteful gold findings. Taken together, the design elements configure into lantern-style earrings with contemporary style and refined elegance.

materials

- 2 faceted, Austrian-crystal cubes, clear, 8mm
- 4 Austrian-crystal bicones, ruby red, 5mm
- 4 round spacer beads, gold, with rhinestones in wine, 6mm dia.
- 2 ball-tipped headpins, gold, 24 gauge, 2" (5.0cm) long
- 2 jump rings, gold, 18 gauge, 6mm dia.
- 1 pair fishhook earrings, ball-and-coil style, gold

tools

- Ruler
- Wire cutters
- 2 chain nose pliers
- Round-nose pliers

techniques

- How to Open and Close a Jump Ring (See pg. 166.)
- How to Make a Wrapped-Wire Loop (See pg. 168.)

Fire and Ice

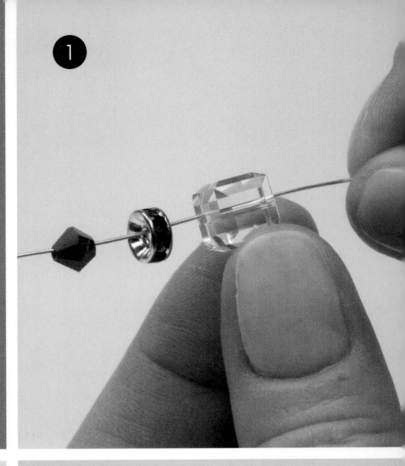

instructions

1.

Insert a headpin into the beads in the following order: one bicone, one spacer, one cube, one spacer, and one bicone.

2.

Make a wrapped-wire loop.

3.

Open one jump ring with both pairs of chain-nose pliers. Thread the jump ring through the wrapped-wire loop and the end of one earring wire. Close the jump ring.

4.

Repeat steps 1-3 to complete the second earring.

2

4

QUICK TIP

These earrings are so quick and easy to make!
Because they only require a few beads,
it's a great project to splurge on Austrian crystals,
semiprecious stones, and real gold
or sterling-silver findings.

Juicy Fruit

EQUAL PARTS TASTY AND TANTALIZING, THE FLAVORFUL "JUICY FRUIT" IS A ONE-OF-A-KIND CHARM BRACELET MADE WITH A FLAT-LINK GOLD CHAIN TO PROVIDE HEFT AND SUBSTANCE. THE ENAMELED CHARMS ARE SHAPED LIKE CHERRIES AND STRAWBERRIES AND GLOW WITH TRANSPARENT COLOR. EACH GLIMMERING PIECE OF FRUIT IS EMBOSSED WITH NATURAL DETAILS AND HIGH-LIGHTED BY STEMS AND LEAVES IN BURNISHED GOLD. A GOLD TOGGLE CLASP ROUNDS OUT THE LOOK OF THIS UTTERLY CHARMING (LITERALLY!) ORIGINAL.

materials

- 8 assorted charms:
  4 cherries, gold-and-red enamel
  4 strawberries, gold-and-red enamel
- 12" (30.4cm) flat-link chain, gold, 12mm, 16mm, oval links
- Toggle clasp, gold, 18mm dia.
- 10 jump rings, gold, 18 gauge, 6mm dia.

tools

- Ruler
- Chain cutters
- 2 chain-nose pliers

techniques

- How to Open and Close a Jump Ring (See pg. 166.)

Juicy Fruit

instructions

1.
Use the chain cutter to cut a 7-in. (17.7cm) length of chain.

2.
Open a jump ring using the chain-nose pliers, and thread it through the last link of the chain and the bar section of the toggle clasp. Close the jump ring. Repeat to attach the hoop section of the toggle clasp to the opposite end of the chain.

3.
Lay the chain bracelet flat on the work surface, making sure there are no twists in the chain. Thread an open jump ring through the loop in a cherry charm.

4.
Thread the jump ring attached to the cherry charm through the first link in the bracelet; close the jump ring. Continue to add charms to the chain, alternating cherries and strawberries, and skipping one link in the chain between them.

QUICK TIP

Charms are available in almost any color and shape imaginable and in any price range. Charms can be made in base metals and colored with enamel, or crafted in gold and silver and set with semiprecious stones. Create a charm bracelet that says something about you and your hopes and dreams.

Sweetheart

Every day is Valentine's Day with this multi-strand necklace that utilizes colorful combinations of red and hot-pink beads. "Sweetheart" is made up of five strands of red bugle beads and four strands of red and hot-pink beads in various styles, shapes, and sizes—red Austrian crystal bicones, round hot-pink beads, flat red discs, and faceted hot-pink oval beads. Striking pink-satin ribbon streamers attach at the back of the neck, adding a touch of elegance and, dare we say...romance?

materials

- 2 pkgs. Austrian-crystal bicones, red, 4mm (Note: One package has approx. 144 bicones.)
- 88 clear round glass beads, hot pink, 8mm dia.
- 13 clear glass discs, red, 1.2cm dia., 2mm thick
- 8 faceted clear oval beads, hot pink, 1cm wide, 1.5cm long
- 1 hank silver-lined crystal bugle beads, red, 2mm dia., 2mm long
- 18 crimp tubes, gold, size 2
- 2 jump rings, gold, 14 gauge, 16mm dia.
- 2 metal findings, gold, 1cm wide, 1.8mm long
- 1 yd. (91.4cm) satin ribbon, hot pink, 1" (2.54cm) wide
- Transite
- Beading wire, 0.32mm dia.
- Cyanoacrylate (instant glue) gel
- White craft glue

tools

- Ruler
- Wire cutters
- Crimping pliers
- 2 chain-nose pliers
- Scissors

techniques

- How to Open and Close a Jump Ring (See pg. 166.)
- How to Use a Crimp Tube/Bead (See pg. 166.)

Finished Length: 20" (50.8cm), adjustable

Sweetheart

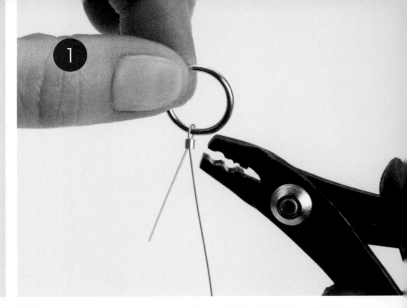

beading patterns

(Bead kinds and sequences for each strand)

A: red bugle beads

B: 4 hot-pink round beads and 4 red bicones; repeat 9 more times

C: red bugle beads

D: 8 hot-pink round beads and 1 hot-pink oval; repeat 4 more times; then add 8 hot-pink round beads

E: red bugle beads

F: 4 red bicones and 1 hot-pink oval; repeat 12 more times; then add 4 red bicones

G: red bugle beads

H: 8 red bicones; 1 red disc; 4 red bicones; repeat 1 disc and 4 bicones 12 more times; then add 8 red bicones

I: red bugle beads

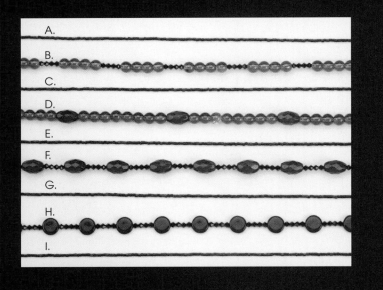

A.

B.

C.

D.

E.

F.

G.

H.

I.

instructions

1.

Use wire cutters to cut nine 22-in. (55.8cm) lengths of beading wire. Use a crimp tube and crimping pliers to attach a 16mm jump ring to the end of one length.

2.

Following the Beading Patterns (opposite), choose one strand and string on the corresponding beads. Thread a crimp tube onto the end of the strand, and attach another 16mm jump ring using the crimping pliers.

3.

Using a crimp tube and the crimping pliers, attach another length of beading wire to the jump ring as in step 1. Follow the directions in step 2 to complete the strand. Continue as before to complete the remaining seven strands. Note: Make certain that the split in the jump ring is opposite the strands of beads.

4.

Lay the beaded strands flat on a work surface. Measure and cut two 8-in. (20.3cm) lengths of transite. Set one aside. Position one gold finding on one jump ring. Note: The finding should cover the crimped ends of the beaded strands. Use the transite to secure the right end of the finding to the right side of the jump ring, tying the transite in a double knot. Trim off the excess transite. Repeat on the left side of the jump ring. Use a small drop of instant glue to secure the knots. Repeat these steps to add the gold finding to the second jump ring.

5.

Thread the satin ribbon through the jump rings, and tie a bow. Trim the ribbon ends on an angle using sharp scissors. Use your finger to carefully apply a thin line of white craft glue to each of the ribbon edges to prevent fraying.

Bubblegum

THINK PINK! BUBBLE-MEETS-BAUBLE IN THESE FUN-AND-FLIRTY DANGLY EARRINGS FASHIONED FROM JADE BRIOLETTES (DYED PINK) AND REFLECTIVE AUSTRIAN-CRYSTAL BICONES IN A BOUNCY-AND-BUBBLY SHADE IN THE PALEST OF PINK. POSITIONED ON TOP OF THE BRIO-LETTES ARE ANTIQUED SILVER FLOWERS WHOSE CEN-TERS GLEAM WITH HOT-PINK RHINESTONES, OFFSETTING THE SILVER EARHOOKS THAT SUSPEND THESE FASHIONABLE CONFECTIONS.

materials

- 2 faceted, opaque dyed-jade briolettes, deep pink, 1.4cm wide, 1.9cm long, 7mm thick
- 2 floral sliders, antique silver with hot-pink rhinestones, 1cm wide, 4mm thick
- 8 Austrian-crystal bicones, light pink, 4mm
- Sterling-silver wire, 22 gauge
- 2 jump rings, silver, 24 gauge, 3mm dia.
- 1 pair fishhook earrings, ball-and-coil style, silver

tools

- Ruler
- Wire cutters
- 2 chain-nose pliers
- Round-nose pliers

techniques

- How to Open and Close a Jump Ring (See pg. 166.)
- How to Make a Wrapped-Wire Loop (See pg. 168.)

Bubblegum

QUICK TIP

Although these earrings can be made in any monochromatic color scheme, also try combining colors such as hot pink, orange, and lime green for a fun, tropical look.

instructions

1.
Use wire cutters to cut two 6-in. (15.2cm) lengths of silver wire. Set one aside. Thread one briolette onto one wire, and slide it to the midpoint. Bend up both ends of the wire.

2.
Thread one light-pink bicone on each wire, followed by one slider and another two light-pink bicones.

3.
Cross the two wire ends.

4.
At the point where the wires cross, use the chain-nose pliers to bend the left wire straight up. Wrap the right wire twice around the straight wire. Use the wire cutters to trim away the excess wrapped wire only.

5.
Use round-nose and chain-nose pliers to make a wrapped-wire loop with the straight wire. Trim away any excess wire.

6.
Open a 3mm jump ring, and thread it through the wrapped-wire loop and one earring wire. Close the jump ring using the chain-nose pliers. Repeat steps 1–6 to complete the second earring.

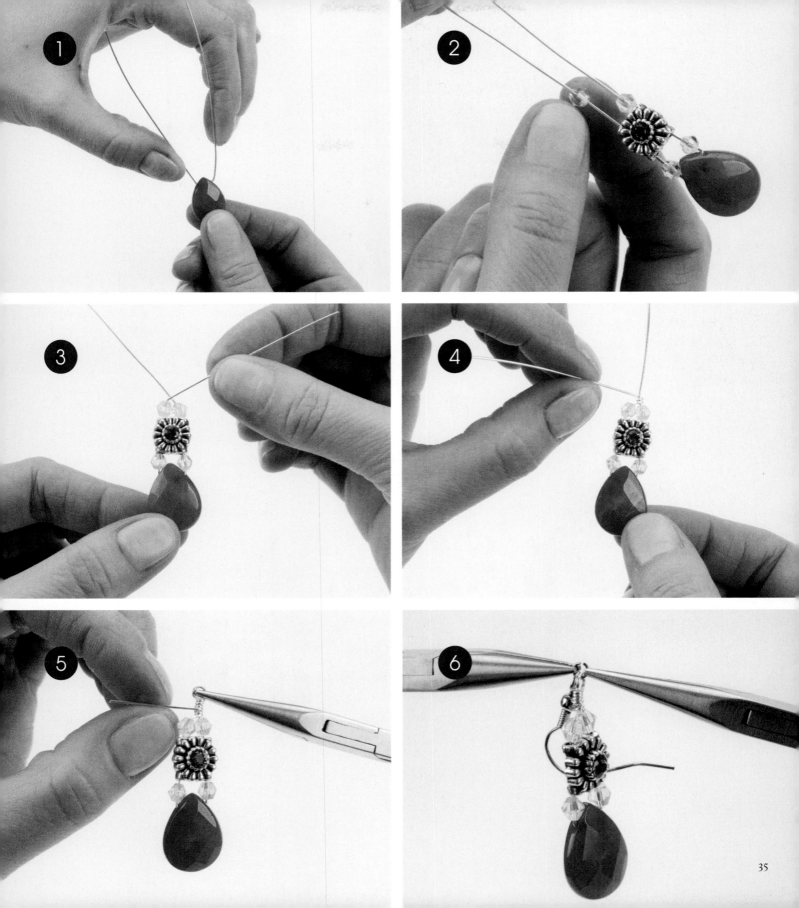

Hibiscus Island

This chunky bracelet with a tropical feel boasts glorious splashes of color. The beautiful "Hibiscus Island" is a three-strand bracelet that is made from polished chunks of coral that are dyed a variegated strawberry red. The wrapped-wire loops that connect the coral beads give the appearance of a floating chain of tropical islands. Gold findings, including a gold spring-ring clasp, are the finishing touches to this modern piece of jewelry that seems to magically transport you to the South Seas.

materials

- 18 flat, dyed-coral ovals, red, 2cm wide, 2.2cm long, 7mm thick
- 2 end bars for 3 strands, gold, 1.8cm long
- 6 jump rings, gold, 18 gauge, 5mm dia.
- 1 jump ring, gold, 16 gauge, 18mm dia.
- 1 jump ring, gold, 18 gauge, 6mm dia.
- 1 spring ring, gold, 18mm dia.
- Gold wire, 22 gauge

tools

- Ruler
- Wire cutters
- 2 chain-nose pliers
- Round-nose pliers

techniques

- How to Open and Close a Jump Ring (See pg. 166)
- How to Make a Wrapped-Wire Loop (See pg. 168.)
- How to Connect Wrapped-Wire Loops to Make a Chain (See page 169.)

Hibiscus Island

instructions

1.

Use 18 coral ovals and gold wire to make three chains of six ovals each. See page 169 for details.

2.

Use chain-nose pliers to open one 5mm jump ring. Thread it through the end loop of one coral chain and one outside hole on an end bar. Repeat with a second 5mm jump ring to attach the opposite end loop of the same coral chain to the corresponding hole on the second end bar.

3.

Repeat step 2 to attach the remaining two coral chains, making sure to attach each end of the chain to the corresponding hole in the end bars.

4.

Use the chain-nose pliers to attach the 18mm jump ring to one end bar. Use the 6mm jump ring on the other side to attach the spring ring to the second end bar.

QUICK TIP

Real coral is available in shades of deep red to pale pink, as well as black, white, blue, and gold. When found in nature, it has a distinctive wood-grain quality and a matte finish; then it is polished to a glossy finish for jewelry-making purposes.

Orange and Yellow

Warm and cheery, orange and yellow are the most upbeat colors in the spectrum. Picture a vase of sunny daffodils or a bowl of bright lemons or tangerines bursting with life and vitality. Yellow symbolizes joy and happiness, while orange is thought to evoke vigor and enthusiasm. These lively, vivid hues are a balm for the emotions. Witness the spirit-lifting powers of a field of sunflowers on a crisp fall day, a monarch butterfly against a cornflower-blue sky, or a canary-yellow slicker against the gray drizzle on a rainy afternoon. Glowing golden candlelight stirs the senses, while shiny gold coins stir the imagination. The golden hues of fall—pumpkin, mustard, rust, and burnished-bronze can stir up a wellspring of emotion.

Orange and yellow are a natural pairing in fashion and décor, as they are in nature. Mix clear, bright shades of orange and yellow with lime green, or hot pink and fuchsia, for a lush, tropical jungle feel. Stones like amber, citrine, golden coral, orange calcite, and smoky topaz can create a rich autumnal fantasy—add some striking blue lapis lazuli for gorgeous contrast. Mixing metallics with warm hues can make you sparkle and shine like a bronzed goddess. Go for fun-and-funky by blending banana-yellow and cantaloupe-coral colors with watermelon pink and deep blueberry for 40s-era kitsch.

Gold Rush

In 1849, a sleepy California valley was abuzz with news that gold had been discovered. No small discovery, the early love affair with this precious metal inspired a rush for gold that has continued ever since. Here, our "Gold Rush" bracelet maximizes the gold effect in a glowing 15-coil cuff made from memory wire that's strung with strands and strands of lustrous gold bugle beads. Never losing its shape or appeal, the luxurious "Gold Rush" bracelet is accented with a rhinestone flower originally designed as a button.

materials

- 1 hank silver-lined crystal bugle beads, gold, 2mm dia., 5mm long
- Memory wire, gold, bracelet weight
- 1 jump ring, 18 gauge, 6mm dia.
- Rhinestone button, amber, 15mm dia.

tools

- Memory wire cutters
- 2 chain-nose pliers
- Emery cloth
- Ruler

techniques

- How to Open and Close a Jump Ring (See pg. 166.)

Gold Rush

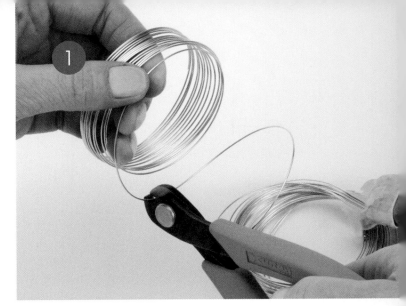

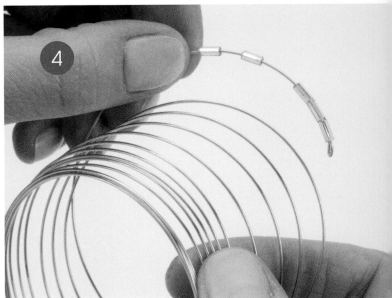

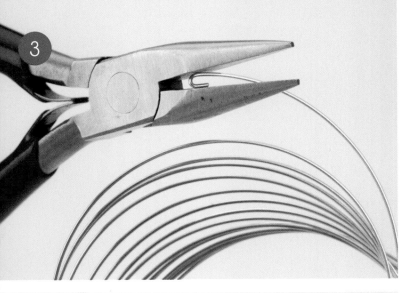

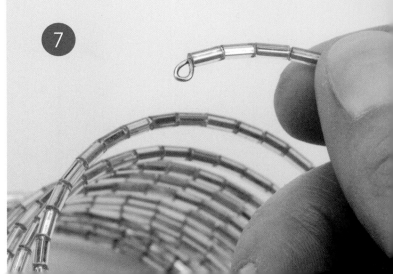

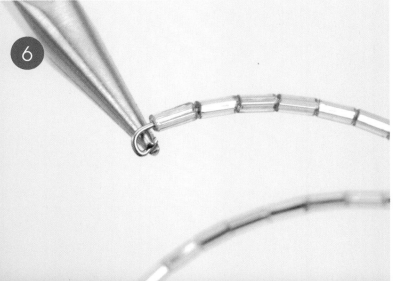

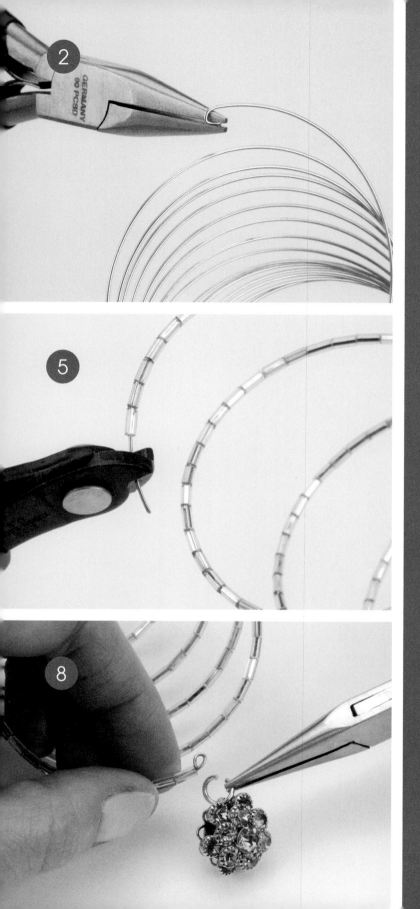

1.
Count 15 complete loops of memory wire,
and use the wire cutters to cut the loops from the coil.
Use emery cloth to smooth the cut ends.

2.
Use the tips of the chain-nose pliers to bend the wire
⅛ in. (3.0mm) from one end.

3.
Use a wider section of the pliers' jaws to squeeze
the end flat to the wire.

4.
Thread the opposite end of the wire through
a few bugle beads. Slide the beads along the wire until
they reach the bent end.

5.
Continue adding beads until there is approximately
1 in. (2.5cm) of wire unbeaded. Measure ¼ in. (6.0mm)
from the last bead. Then use the wire
cutters to remove the excess wire.

6.
Use the chain-nose pliers to bend the end of the wire into
a loop. Note: Do not squeeze the end flat as in step 3.

7.
Use the chain-nose pliers to continue to shape the loop so
the end of the wire touches the main wire as shown.
Note: The loop is created to secure the beads and to allow
the decorative button to be attached.

8.
Open the jump ring using both pairs of chain-nose pliers.
Thread one end through the button and the loop end of
the bracelet created in step 6. Close the jump ring.

Queen Bee

The impressive "Queen Bee" is dripping with style. Sweet and tempting as nature's nectar, this necklace is fashioned from quartz chips in a warm citrine color. Its dazzling, rough-cut citrine pendant in deep amber is combined with a faceted rondelle that mimics the appearance of a shapely and succulent drop of golden honey. Glittering gold findings make this queen as regal as any royal.

materials

- 2 strands of quartz chips, citrine, 6mm wide, 4mm long, 6mm thick (Note: A 16-in.(40.6cm) strand has approximately 135 chips.)
- 1 faceted rough-cut citrine nugget, deep amber, 1.8cm wide, 2.5cm long, 1.2cm thick
- 1 faceted citrine rondelle, amber, 1cm dia., 8mm long
- 2 clamshells, gold
- 2 crimp tubes, gold, size 2
- 1 jump ring, gold, 18 gauge, 7mm dia.
- 1 lobster clasp, gold, 1.5cm long
- 1 headpin, gold, 18 gauge, 5cm long
- Transite

tools

- Ruler
- Wire cutters
- Crimping pliers
- 2 chain-nose pliers
- Round-nose pliers

techniques

- How to Open and Close a Jump Ring (See pg. 166.)
- How to Use a Crimp Tube/Bead (See pg. 166.)
- How to Use a Clamshell (See pg. 167.)
- How to Attach a Clamshell (See pg. 167.)
- How to Use a Clamshell to Cover a Crimp Tube/Bead (See pg. 167.)
- How to Make a Wrapped-Wire Loop (See pg.168)

Finished length: 18" (45.7cm)

Queen Bee

instructions

1.
Use wire cutters to cut one 26-in. (66.0cm) length of transite. Thread one end through one clamshell, one crimp tube, and the lobster clasp. Secure the lobster clasp to the transite using the crimp tube and crimping pliers.

2.
Position the clamshell over the crimp tube, and secure it using pliers. Thread on 150 quartz chips, hiding the end of the transite inside the beads.

3.
Thread on one clamshell, one crimp tube, and the jump ring. Secure the jump ring to the transite using the crimp tube and crimping pliers. Cover the crimp tube with the clamshell. Thread the excess transite inside the last beads to hide it.

4.
To make the pendant, insert the headpin through the nugget and the rondelle.

5.
To begin the wrapped loop, use the chain-nose pliers to grasp the headpin 1/8 in. (3.0mm) above the rondelle. Hold the beads with the other hand, and turn the pliers away from you to bend the headpin stem at a 90-deg. angle. Use the round-nose pliers to grasp the headpin at the bend. Use your fingers to bend the headpin stem around the jaw of the pliers, and cross at the front of the stem to make a loop. Slip the loop over the centerpoint of the necklace between two chips.

6.
Grasp the loop with the chain-nose pliers, and use the second pair of chain-nose pliers to wrap the headpin end around the stem, making a wrapped-wire loop.

Sunset Boulevard

Dazzling like the thousands of lights that line one of the world's most popular thoroughfares, the luminous "Sunset Boulevard" boasts a floral clasp and four strands of beads in glowing shades of red, orange, and yellow. No two strands are the same. Austrian-crystal bicones in Indian and tomato red surround faceted discs in a luscious melon color and variegated beads in shades of incandescent orange. Round beads in coral and champagne, seed beads in orange, and citrine-colored briolettes faithfully reproduce the colors of a glorious California sunset. Beads of sea green and turquoise provide contrast and add an unexpected element of surprise.

materials

- 112 seed beads, metallic gold, size 11
- 23 Austrian-crystal bicones, Indian red, 4mm
- 22 faceted, clear round glass beads, coral, 6mm dia.
- 16 faceted opaque glass discs, melon, 7mm dia., 2mm thick
- 9 clear round glass beads, variegated orange, 8mm dia.
- 8 faceted clear quartz briolettes, citrine, 6mm dia.,12mm long
- 7 faceted, clear round glass beads, champagne, 8mm dia.
- 6 clear round glass beads, sea green, 3mm dia.
- 6 Austrian-crystal bicones, tomato red, 4mm
- 4 faceted Austrian-crystal rondelles, turquoise, 4mm dia.
- 3 seed beads, orange, size 11
- 3 faceted Austrian-crystal ovals, baby pink, 6mm wide, 8mm thick
- 8 crimp tubes, gold, size 2
- 1 floral clasp, for three strands, gold, 1cm dia.
- Beading wire, 0.32mm dia.

tools

- Ruler
- Wire cutters
- Crimping pliers

techniques

- How to Use a Crimp Tube/Bead (See pg. 166.)

Sunset Boulevard

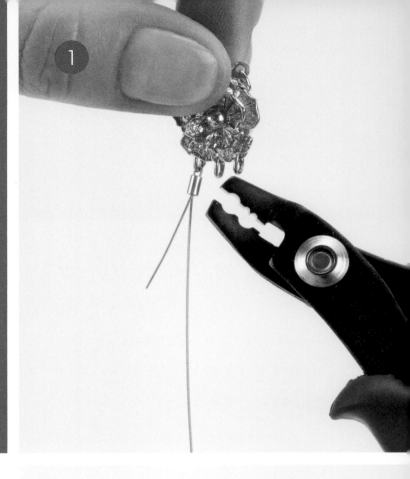

instructions

1.

Use the wire cutters to cut four 12-in. (30.4cm) lengths of beading wire. Attach one strand of beading wire to an outside hole on the floral clasp using a crimp tube and crimping pliers.

2.

Thread on several beads following the Beading Layout (opposite) or as desired, hiding the end of the beading wire inside the beads. String on the remaining beads, finishing the desired sequence.

3.

Use a crimp bead and the crimping pliers to attach the end of the strand to the corresponding outside hole in the second part of the clasp. Tuck the wire end inside the last beads.

4.

Repeat steps 1-3 to bead the remaining three strands, attaching two strands to the center hole and the fourth strand to the remaining outside hole of each section of the clasp.

Beading Layout

Monarch Butterfly

The magnificent "Monarch Butterfly" is a pretty duo of bracelets that uses the same beading technique to create two different looks. The bracelets can be worn separately or together. One bracelet is a monocrhomatic beauty crafted from simple orange-glass beads with a matte finish. The companion bracelet boasts shapely lampwork beads in black, white, and orange. Small glass beads in radiant orange separate the lampwork beads, and a gold clasp adds extra sparkle.

materials

Bracelet 1 (opposite left)
- 14 lampwork beads, orange, white, and black, 14mm dia.
- 15 round glass beads, orange, 4mm dia.
- 2 crimp tubes, gold, size 2
- 1 jump ring, gold, 18 gauge, 6mm dia.
- 1 lobster clasp, gold, 1.4cm long
- Beading wire, 0.32mm dia.

Bracelet 2 (opposite right)
- 20 opaque matte glass beads, orange, 10mm dia.
- 2 crimp tubes, gold, size 2
- 1 jump ring, gold, 18 gauge, 6mm dia.
- 1 lobster clasp, gold, 1.4cm long
- Beading wire, 0.32mm dia.

tools

- Ruler
- Wire cutters
- Chain-nose pliers
- Crimping pliers

techniques

- How to Use a Crimp Tube/Bead (See pg. 166.)

Monarch Butterfly

instructions

(bracelet 1)

1a.
Use the wire cutters to cut one 12-in. (30.3cm) length of beading wire. Use a crimp tube and crimping pliers to attach a lobster clasp to one end of the beading wire.

2a.
Thread the opposite end of the wire through one round 4mm orange bead and one lampwork bead. Hide the wire end inside the beads.

3a.
Thread on the remaining beads, alternating the orange and the lampwork beads. Use a crimp tube and crimping pliers to attach a jump ring to the end of the wire. Hide the wire inside the last beads; trim off the excess.

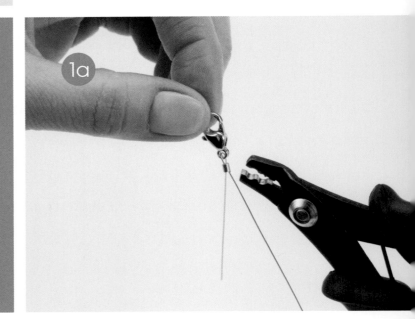

(bracelet 2)

1b.
Use the wire cutters to cut one 12-in. (30.3cm) length of beading wire. Use a crimp tube and crimping pliers to attach a lobster clasp to one end of the beading wire.

2b.
Thread the opposite end of the wire through 20 matte-orange beads. Hide the ends of the beading wire inside the beads.

3b.
Use a crimp tube and crimping pliers to attach a jump ring to the end of the beading wire, hiding the wire inside the last beads and trimming away the excess.

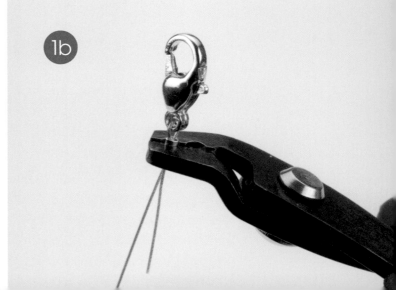

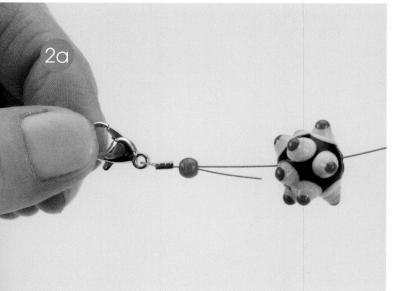

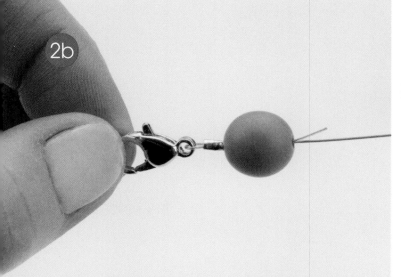

Tutti Frutti

Mmmmm. The multicolored "Tutti Frutti" necklace looks (almost) good enough to eat—like a sugary, sweet candy necklace or a cool and refreshing melon dessert. This charming little necklace features two strands of beads in various sizes and colors—juicy orange, cantaloupe, watermelon pink, and sunburst yellow. Its breezy tropical mix of fruit-colored beads features a repeating design, so it's easy to make. The necklace is finished with a simple barrel clasp in gold.

materials

- 82 round dyed-coral beads, cantaloupe, 4mm dia.
- 82 round glass beads, orange, 4mm dia.
- 42 round dyed-coral beads, pink, 5mm dia.
- 42 faceted dyed-jade rondelles, yellow, 6mm dia., 4mm long
- 4 crimp beads, gold, size 2
- 1 barrel clasp, gold, 4mm wide, 8mm long
- Beading wire, 0.32mm dia.

tools

- Ruler
- Wire cutters
- Chain-nose pliers
- Crimping pliers

techniques

- How to Use a Crimp Tube/Bead (See pg. 166.)

Finished length: 20" (50.8cm)

Tutti Frutti

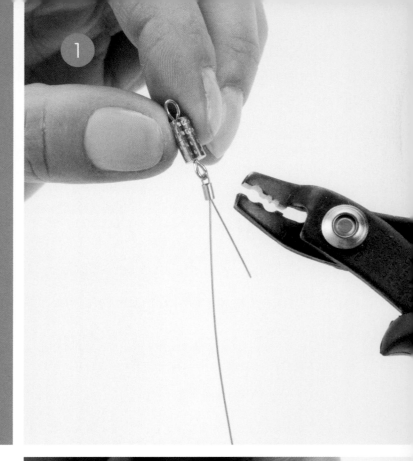

instructions

1.
Use the wire cutters to cut two 28-in. (70.8cm) length of beading wire. Set one aside. Use a crimp tube and crimping pliers to attach the end of one length of beading wire to one end of the barrel clasp.

2.
Divide each type of bead into two equal groups. Move one group aside. Thread on the beads in the group following the Beading Pattern (circular inset) or as desired. Hide the end of the wire inside the beads.

3.
Use a crimp tube and crimping pliers to attach the end of the beading wire to the second part of the barrel clasp. Tuck the wire end into the last beads. Trim away any excess wire.

4.
Repeat steps 1–3 to attach the second strand of beads to the barrel clasp.

Beading Pattern

STYLE TIP

For a pretty ensemble, make the "Carmen Miranda" earrings pictured above and featured on page 63.

Carmen Miranda

"Festive" and "fun" are the words that best describe these distinctive earrings inspired by the famed "Lady in the Tutti Frutti Hat." Flashy and flavorful, these baubles look great when paired with, appropriately, the "Tutti Frutti" necklace (featured on page 59). In "Carmen Miranda," brightly colored beads in cantaloupe, watermelon pink, and yellow are attached to a faceted briolette in iridescent tangerine. Each small, round bead features a wrapped-wire loop, and the beads are clustered on a jump ring that allows them to jump and dance about like the vivacious 1940s entertainer who gives these sparkly danglers their name.

materials

- 8 round dyed-coral beads, cantaloupe, 4mm dia.
- 4 round dyed-coral beads, pink, 5mm dia.
- 4 faceted dyed-jade rondelles, yellow, 6mm dia., 4mm long
- 2 faceted, iridescent quartz briolettes, tangerine, 1.3cm wide, 1.8cm long, 5mm thick
- 16 headpins, gold, 24 gauge, 3cm long
- 2 jump rings, gold, 18 gauge, 6mm dia.
- 1 pair fishhook earrings, ball-and-coil style, gold
- Gold wire, 24 gauge

tools

- Ruler
- Wire cutters
- 2 chain-nose pliers
- Round-nose pliers

techniques

- How to Open and Close a Jump Ring (See pg. 166.)
- How to Make a Wrapped-Wire Loop (See pg. 168.)

Carmen Miranda

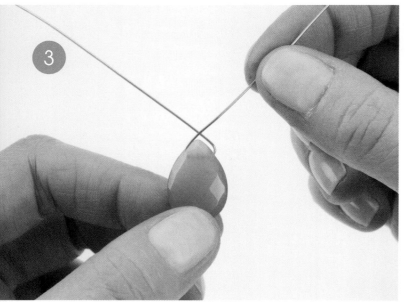

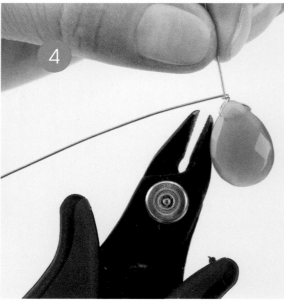

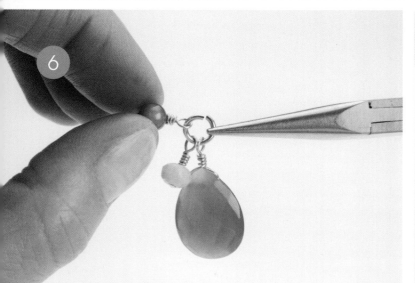

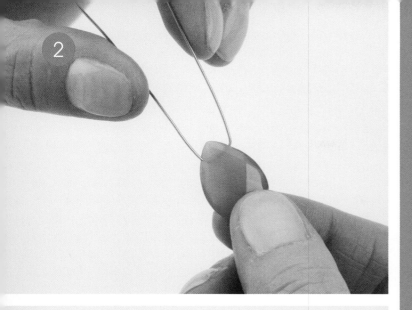

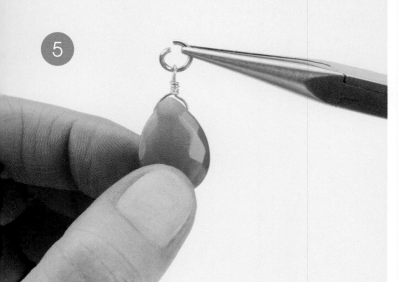

instructions

1.
Insert a headpin through one pink bead.
Use the round-nose pliers to make a wrapped-wire loop.
Repeat to add wrapped-wire loops to one pink bead,
two yellow beads, and four cantaloupe beads. Set the
bead units aside.

2.
Use wire cutters to cut two 6-in. (15.2cm) lengths of gold
wire. Set one length aside. Thread the end of other wire
through one briolette, and slide it to the midpoint of the
wire. Bend up both ends of the wire.

3.
Cross the two wires at the tip of the briolette as shown.

4.
At the point where the wires cross, use the chain-nose
pliers to bend the left wire straight. Wrap the right wire
twice around the straight wire. Use the wire cutters to trim
away the excess wrapped wire only.

5.
Use the round-nose pliers to make a wrapped-wire loop
with the straight wire. Trim away any excess wire. Use both
chain-nose pliers to open a jump ring. Thread one end
through the wrapped-wire loop.

6.
Hold the open jump ring with one pair of the chain-nose
pliers. Referring to the Beading Layout (left), thread on
four bead units from step 1 on one side of the jump ring.
Then move the pliers to the opposite side of the
jump ring, and thread on the remaining four bead units.

7.
Thread one earring wire onto the jump ring.
Close the jump ring using the chain-nose pliers.
Repeat steps 1–7 to complete the second earring.

Beading Layout

Green

GREEN IS THE COLOR OF NATURE, GROWTH, AND NEW LIFE: ENVISION SPRINGTIME FIELDS OF NEW GREEN GRASS, CHARTREUSE BUDS ON WOODY BRANCHES, AND TURTLES PADDLING IN BOTTLE-GREEN PONDS. GREEN IS CLEAR, FRESH, AND INVIGORATING: A SEA-FOAM GREEN SWIMMING POOL ON A HOT SUMMER DAY, A TWIST OF LIME IN A MINT MOJITO, OR A SWEEP OF EVERGREEN BRANCHES ON NEW-FALLEN SNOW. GREEN IS THE ONLY COLOR THAT IS ALSO A SCENT: PERFUMERS DESCRIBE CERTAIN FRESH, GRASSY, OR PINE-LIKE FRAGRANCES AS "GREEN," AND IT'S EASY TO SEE WHY. LIKE BLUE, GREEN CAN BE RELAXING AND SOOTHING TO THE EYE AND THE SENSES—PRACTITIONERS OF FENG SHUI USE THE COLOR GREEN TO CONFER A SENSE OF PEACE AND HARMONY TO A SPACE AND TO INVOKE PROSPERITY. GREEN CAN BE YOUTHFUL, FLIRTY, AND FUN: PICTURE A KELLY-GREEN SHAMROCK PAINTED ON A CHEEK FOR ST. PATRICK'S DAY. GREEN CAN BE AS SPORTY AS A GREEN ON A GOLF COURSE, AS FLASHY AS A TRAFFIC LIGHT, OR AS TRANQUIL AS A CUP OF GREEN TEA.

GREEN COMBINES WELL WITH A MULTITUDE OF OTHER COLORS, DEPENDING ON ITS SHADE. YELLOW GREENS, SUCH AS LIME AND CHARTREUSE, MIX WELL WITH WARM TONES, SUCH AS ORANGE OR YELLOW, FOR A FRESH, FRUITY PALETTE. DEEP HUNTER OR JADE GREEN PAIRED WITH EARTHY BROWN AND PALE BLUE—THINK AQUAMARINE—PRODUCES ECHOES OF A FOREST STREAM. FOR A SPORTY LOOK, MIX KELLY GREEN WITH BLACK AND WHITE, OR FOR A PREPPY COMBO, MIX GREEN WITH BUBBLE-GUM PINK.

English Garden

'Corvedale', 'Christopher Marlowe', 'Ambridge Rose', these are just some of the names of the rose varieties found in a quaint English Garden. Likewise, these single-strand bracelets offer some impressively crafted flowers of their own. Delicate pink roses, hand-painted on round, light-green beads are combined with Austrian-crystal bicones and green-and-pink lampwork beads to create an air of elegance and sophistication. A second single-strand bracelet boasts plump discs in emerald green that frame lampwork beads in deep pink with accents in molten glass. Silver findings—a magnetic clasp and crimp covers—put the finishing touches on this aristocratic charmer.

materials

Bracelet 1 (opposite left)
- 7 round painted-glass beads, green with pink roses, 12mm dia.
- 7 lampwork discs, light green, white and pink, 14mm dia., 7mm thick
- 15 Austrian-crystal bicones, 6mm
- 2 crimp tubes, silver, size 2
- 2 crimp covers, silver
- 1 magnetic barrel clasp, silver, 8mm long
- Beading wire, 0.32mm dia.

Bracelet 2 (opposite right)
- 8 lampwork discs, dark pink, white and green, 1.5cm dia., 9mm thick
- 16 clear glass discs, green, 1cm dia., 6mm thick
- 9 Austrian-crystal bicones, light green, 6mm
- 2 crimp tubes, silver, size 2
- 2 crimp covers, silver
- 1 magnetic barrel clasp, silver, 8mm long
- Beading wire, 0.32mm dia.

tools

- Ruler
- Wire cutters
- Chain-nose pliers,
- Crimping pliers

techniques

- How to Use a Crimp Tube/Bead (See pg. 166.)
- How to Use a Crimp Cover (See pg. 166.)

English Garden

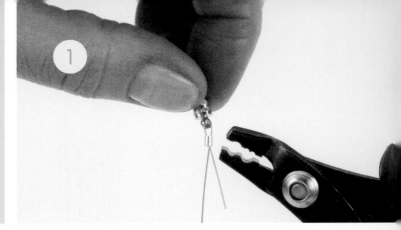

HELPFUL TIP

Using a magnetic clasp to finish a bracelet makes putting it on really easy. Just make sure that the clasp that you choose can support the weight of the beads you're using.

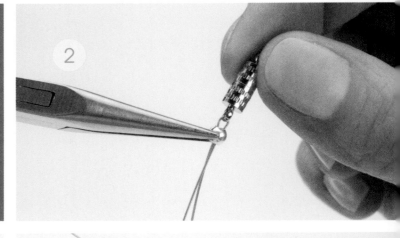

instructions (bracelet 1) >

1.
Use wire cutters to cut one 12-in. (30.5cm) length of beading wire. Use a crimp tube and crimping pliers to attach the wire to one end of the barrel clasp.

2.
Cover the crimp tube with a crimp cover.

3.
Thread the opposite end of the wire through one pink crystal, one lampwork disc, one pink crystal, and one painted-glass bead. Hide the end of the wire inside the beads. Thread on the remaining beads in the sequence shown or as desired. Tuck the wire end into the last beads.

4.
Use a crimp tube and crimping pliers to attach the end of the beading wire to the opposite end of the barrel clasp. Tuck the wire end into the last beads. Cover the crimp tube with a crimp cover.

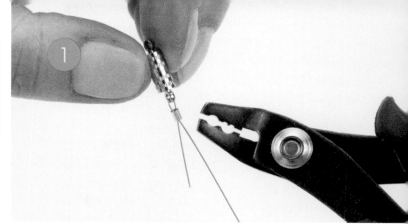

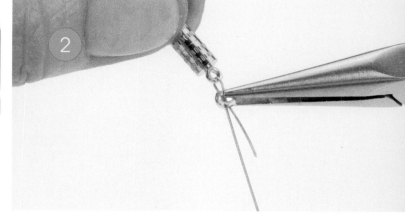

instructions (bracelet 2) >

1.

Use wire cutters to cut one 12-in. (30.5cm) length of beading wire. Use a crimp tube and crimping pliers to attach the wire to one end of the barrel clasp.

2.

Cover the crimp tube with a crimp cover.

3.

Thread the opposite end of the wire through one green bicone crystal, one green disc, one dark-pink lampwork disc, and one green disc. Hide the end of the wire inside the beads. Thread on the remaining beads in the sequence shown or as desired. Tuck the wire end into the last beads.

4.

Use a crimp tube and crimping pliers to attach the end of the beading wire to the opposite end of the barrel clasp. Tuck the wire end into the last beads. Cover the crimp tube with a crimp cover.

Sea Grass

"A LEAF OF GRASS IS NO LESS THAN THE JOURNEY-WORK OF THE STARS," SAID THE POET WALT WHITMAN. THIS SHIMMERING, IRIDESCENT SINGLE-STRAND NECKLACE COMBINES THE SUN-BLEACHED GREEN OF WILD REEDS WITH THE SOOTHING BLUE OF A ROLLING SEA. FACETED ROUND BEADS IN AQUA BLUE OFFSET CIRCULAR, FLAT DISCS FASHIONED FROM SHELLS DYED LUMINOUS GREEN. THE NECKLACE IS FINISHED WITH A SHINY SILVER-BALL CLASP. THE "SEA GRASS" NECKLACE IS SO EVOCATIVE OF THE OCEAN THAT YOU CAN PRACTICALLY HEAR THE RUSH OF THE TIDE AND THE CRY OF THE GULLS.

materials

- 27 opaque dyed-shell discs, green, 1.2cm dia., 4mm thick
- 28 faceted, opaque round beads, aqua, 4mm dia.
- 2 crimp beads, silver, size 2
- 2 crimp covers, silver
- 1 round ball clasp, sterling silver, 1cm dia.

tools

- Ruler
- Wire cutters
- Chain-nose pliers
- Crimping pliers

techniques

- How to Use a Crimp Tube/Bead (See pg. 166.)
- How to Use a Crimp-Cover (See pg. 166.)

Finished Length: 18" (45.7cm)

Sea Grass

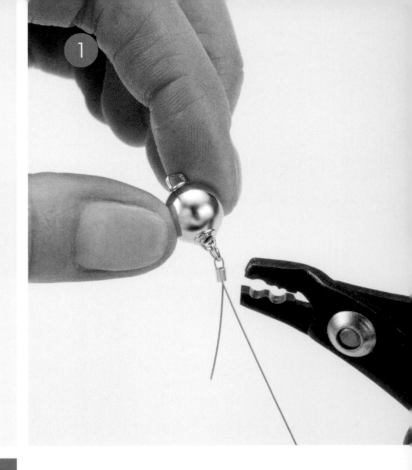

instructions

1.
Use wire cutters to cut one 24-in. (60.0cm) length of beading wire. Attach one end of the wire to one end of the ball clasp using a crimp tube and crimping pliers.

2.
Cover the crimp bead with a crimp cover.

3.
Thread the opposite end of the wire through one aqua-blue bead and one green shell disc. Hide the end of the beading wire inside the beads. Continue beading, alternating the aqua-blue and the green beads using the remaining beads. End with an aqua-blue bead.

4.
Use a crimp tube and crimping pliers to attach the end of the beading wire to the opposite end of the ball clasp. Tuck the wire end into the last beads, snipping off any extra. Cover the crimp bead with a crimp cover.

2

4

HELPFUL TIP

It is not necessary to use a crimp cover—
it is strictly decorative. But it is often
the small finishing touches that distinguish
fine workmanship.

Jungle Parrot

There may be over 300 species of parrots in the wild, but the "Jungle Parrot" bracelet is quite a rare bird indeed. Made from a foundation of two coils of memory wire, the fanciful and exotic "Jungle Parrot" is a real showoff, its uniquely-shaped lime-green paddle beads radiating in a random pattern of "feathers." Paddle beads are similar to dagger beads but are molded into paddle shapes that resemble brightly colored feathers, whereas dagger beads are shaped like kernels of rice. "Jungle Parrot" can be made with dagger beads for a less funky effect.

materials

- 152 opaque glass paddle beads, lime, 9mm wide, 18mm long, 3mm thick
- Memory wire, silver, bracelet weight

tools

- Ruler
- Memory-wire cutters
- Chain-nose pliers
- Emery cloth

Jungle Parrot

instructions

1.
Count two complete loops of memory wire, and use the wire cutters to cut the loops from the coil. Use emery cloth to smooth the cut ends.

2.
Use the tips of the chain-nose pliers to bend the wire ⅛ in. (3.0mm) from one end.

3.
Use a wider section of the pliers' jaws to squeeze the end flat to the wire.

4.
Thread the opposite end of the wire through a few paddle beads. Slide the beads along the wire until they reach the bent end.

5.
Continue adding beads until there is approximately 1 in. (2.5cm) of wire unbeaded. Measure ¼ in. (6.0mm) from the last bead. Then use the wire cutters to trim off the excess wire.

6.
Use the tips of the chain-nose pliers to bend the end of the wire as in step 2.

7.
Repeat step 3 to finish the bracelet.

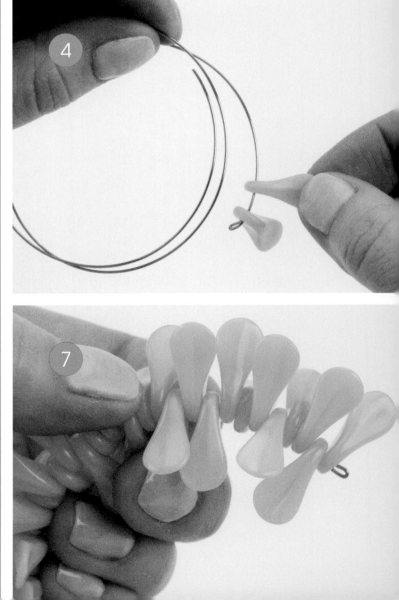

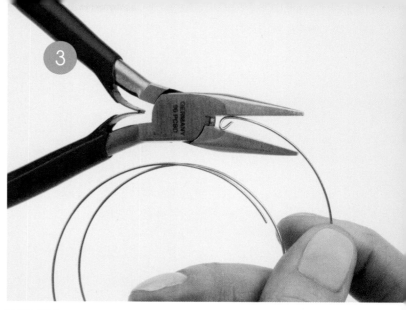

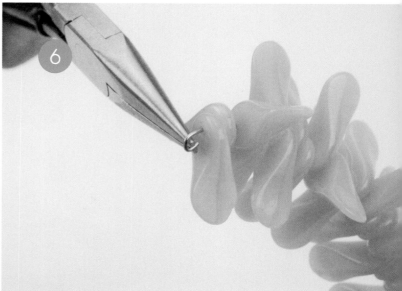

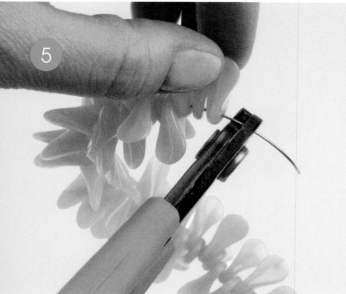

79

HELPFUL TIP

Using only paddle beads on a bracelet or necklace creates a unique ruffled effect. For added interest, mix paddle beads in different colors, such as lime, orange, and hot pink.

Spring Blossom

Spring has sprung! With its verdant color and "flower" centerpiece in full-bloom, this playful bracelet glows with the various green shades of the season. "Spring Blossom" is composed of round beads in fancy jasper and lime green, faceted quartz rondelles in jade and sea-foam green, and faceted accent beads in peridot and aquamarine, each "blooming" on a link of the sterling-silver chain. The main attraction of "Spring Blossom" is a delicate flower composed of five "petals" made from faceted, flat briolettes. A single bead made from turquoise (dyed a cheerful lime-green color) is situated in the center of the blossom, highlighting the milky sheen of each petal. An attractive toggle clasp secures this seasonal charmer.

materials

- 5 faceted dyed-quartz briolettes, sea-foam green, 16mm wide, 26mm long, 9mm thick
- 9 faceted dyed-quartz rondelles, jade green, 12mm dia., 8mm thick
- 9 faceted glass rondelles, peridot, 8mm dia., 4mm thick
- 3 faceted dyed-quartz rondelles, dark sea-foam green, 15mm dia., 11mm thick
- 3 iridescent round glass beads, aquamarine, 6mm dia.
- 8 round dyed-turquoise beads, lime green, 10mm dia.
- 7 round glass beads, fancy jasper, 10mm dia.
- 2 jump rings, sterling silver, 18 gauge, 6mm dia.
- 27 jump rings, sterling silver, 18 gauge, 7mm dia.
- Toggle clasp, sterling silver, 15mm dia.
- 7" (17.8cm) cable-link chain, sterling silver, 8mm wide, 10mm links
- 26 headpins, sterling silver
- Wire, sterling silver, 20 gauge
- Transite

tools

- Ruler
- Wire cutters
- 2 chain-nose pliers
- Round-nose pliers

techniques

- How to Open and Close a Jump Ring (See pg. 166.)
- How to Make a Wrapped-Wire Loop (See page 168)
- How to Make a Beaded Flower (See pg. 171.)

Spring Blossom

Beading Layout

instructions

1.

Use chain-nose pliers and one 6mm jump ring to attach the bar section of the toggle clasp to one end of the silver chain. Use the second 6mm jump ring to attach the hoop section of the toggle clasp to the opposite end of the chain.

2.

To make one bead unit C: insert one headpin through one jade-green rondelle and one peridot rondelle. Make a wrapped-wire loop. Set the bead unit aside.

3.

Refer to the photo, then make one bead unit A: insert a headpin through one fancy jasper bead, and make a wrapped-wire loop; repeat to make six more bead unit As. Make one bead unit B: insert a headpin through one lime-green bead, and make a wrapped-wire loop; repeat to make six more bead unit Bs. Make eight more bead unit Cs as in step 2. Make one bead unit D: insert one headpin through one dark sea-foam green rondelle and one aquamarine glass bead, and make a wrapped-wire loop; repeat to make two more bead unit Ds.

4.

Assemble the sea-foam green briolettes and a lime-green bead into the "flower" as shown here. Set the flower aside.

5.

Thread an open jump ring through the wrapped-wire loop on a lime-green bead. Open a jump ring and use it to attach the bead to the chain as shown. Close the jump ring. Continue adding beads to the chain, following the Beading Layout (opposite).

6.

Thread an open jump ring through the wire loop on the back of the beaded flower. Attach the flower to the center link in the chain, moving some of the beads aside. Close the jump ring.

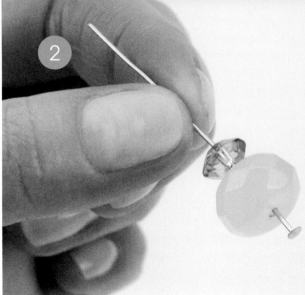

A.   B.   C.   D.

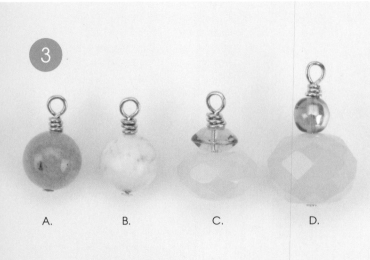

Olive Martini

H. L. MENCKEN CALLED THE MARTINI "THE ONLY AMERICAN INVENTION AS PERFECT AS THE SONNET," BUT THIS APPETIZING CONCOCTION OF SPARKLING BEADS CERTAINLY COMES CLOSE. EQUAL PARTS FLASH AND FINESSE, "OLIVE MARTINI" IS A PAIR OF DELICIOUS DROP EARRINGS COMPOSED OF A DELICATE GOLD CHAIN WITH A LARGE, FACETED NUGGET IN SMOKY QUARTZ. SUSPENDED DRAMATICALLY ABOVE THE NUGGET ARE CLUSTERS OF SMALLER BEADS IN DIFFERENT SIZES, SHAPES, AND COLORS, INCLUDING APPLE GREEN, CELERY, MOSS, JADE, AND FITTINGLY, OLIVE GREEN. AN ELEGANT TREASURE THAT SHARES ITS NAME WITH THE WORLD'S MOST ELEGANT COCKTAIL, "OLIVE MARTINI" EARRINGS ARE SMART, SEXY, AND SMOOTH.

materials

- 2 faceted smoky-quartz nuggets, 1cm wide, 1.8mm long, 8mm thick
- 4 Austrian-crystal bicones, apple green, 6mm
- 2 faceted Austrian-crystal round beads, celery green, 6mm dia.
- 2 faceted Austrian-crystal round beads, moss green, 6mm dia.
- 2 round new-jade beads, light green, 6mm dia.
- 2 faceted new-jade beads, light green, 6mm dia.
- 4 faceted Austrian-crystal round beads, moss green, 4mm dia.
- 4 round new jade beads, light green, 4mm dia.
- 4 faceted Austrian-crystal round beads, celery green, 4mm dia.
- 6 round jade beads, green, 4mm dia.
- 2 faceted Austrian-crystal round beads, moss green, 3mm dia.
- 8 Austrian-crystal bicones, olive green, 4mm dia.
- Cable-link chain, gold, 24-gauge round wire, 2mm wide, 2mm long
- 42 headpins, gold, 4cm long
- 2 jump rings, gold, 20 gauge, 3mm dia.
- 1 pair leverback earring, gold, 1cm wide, 1.4cm long

tools

- Ruler, wire cutters, 2 chain-nose pliers, round-nose pliers

techniques

- How to Open and Close a Jump Ring (See pg. 166.)
- How to Make an Eye Loop (See pg. 170.)
- How to Open and Close an Eye Loop (See pg. 169.)

Olive Martini

instructions

1.
Use wire cutters to cut two 1-in. (2.5cm) lengths of chain. Set one length aside.

2.
Open one jump ring, and thread one end through the end link of the chain and one earring. Close the jump ring. Set the earring aside.

3.
Divide each type of bead into two halves. Move one set of halves aside. Insert one headpin through one smoky-quartz nugget. Make an eye loop.

4.
Open the eye loop using the chain-nose pliers. Slip the end link at the loose end of the chain (set aside in step 2) onto the eye loop on the nugget. Close the eye loop.

5.
Use headpins to make eye loops on each of the remaining beads, following the Beading Pattern (opposite). Then, open the eye loop on one bead using the chain-nose pliers, and thread it through one link on the chain above the smoky-quartz nugget. Close the eye loop.

6.
Repeat step 5 to attach the rest of the beads to the chain in a random pattern or as desired. Repeat steps 2–6 to make the second earring.

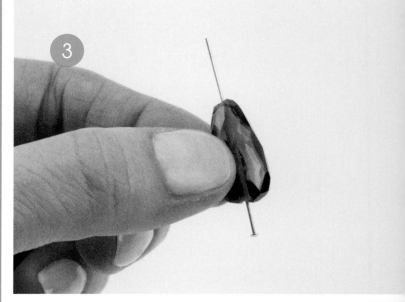

Beading Pattern

Emerald City

The precious, luminescent emerald, first mined by the Ancient Egyptians, lends its name to this single-strand necklace made from Czech cut-crystal beads in a rich metallic emerald green. Faceted gold beads sit between the green gems, creating a pleasing symmetrical design with graduating beads—smaller beads situated near the clasp. The main attraction of "Emerald City" is a drop pendant made from a faceted briolette in smoky quartz. The stunning "Emerald City" is set off with gold findings and a toggle clasp.

materials

- 1 faceted smoky-quartz briolette, 3cm wide, 4cm long, 4mm thick
- 24 faceted round metallic Czech cut-crystal beads, emerald green, 8mm dia.
- 25 faceted round metallic Czech cut-crystal beads, emerald green, 6mm dia.
- 13 faceted round Czech cut-crystal beads, gold, 4mm dia.
- 16 faceted round Czech cut-crystal beads, gold, 2mm dia.
- 2 faceted round metallic Czech cut-crystal beads, emerald green, 2mm dia.
- 2 crimp tubes, gold, size 2
- 1 jump ring, gold, 18 gauge, 5mm dia.
- Toggle clasp, gold, 1.5cm dia.
- Beading wire, 0.32mm dia.
- Transite
- Cyanoacrylate (instant glue) gel

tools

- Ruler
- Wire cutters
- 2 chain-nose pliers

techniques

- How to Open and Close a Jump Ring (See pg. 166.)
- How to Use a Crimp Tube/Bead (See pg. 166.)

Finished length: 18" (45.7cm)

Emerald City

instructions

1.

Use wire cutters to cut a 26-in. (66.0cm) length of beading wire. Use a crimp tube and crimping pliers to attach the hoop section of the toggle clasp to one end of the beading wire.

2.

Thread on one 2mm gold bead and two 6mm emerald beads; repeat five more times. Hide the end of the beading wire inside the beads. Thread on one 4mm gold bead and two 8mm emerald beads; repeat 11 more times. Thread on one 4mm gold bead. Thread on two 6mm emerald beads and one 2mm gold bead; repeat five more times.

3.

Use a crimp tube and crimping pliers to attach the jump ring to the end of the strand. Hide the end of the wire inside the last few beads. Open the jump ring. Thread one end of the jump ring through the loop on the bar section of the toggle clasp. Close the jump ring.

4.

Cut a 6-in. (15.2cm) length of transite for the pendant. Thread the transite through the hole in the quartz pendant, pulling the ends of the transite even. String on one 2mm gold bead, one 2mm emerald bead, and one 2mm gold bead on each side of the pendant.

5.

Bring the ends of the transite together, and thread them through one 6mm emerald bead, sliding the bead towards the pendant.

6.

Wrap both ends of the transite around the center gold bead on the necklace, one end to the right of the bead, and one end to the left.

7.

Thread the ends back through the emerald bead. Adjust the transite so that the emerald bead sits just below the center gold bead.

8.

Tie a double-overhand knot below the emerald bead. Trim away the excess transite. Place a drop of glue on the knot to secure it. Hide the knot in the emerald bead.

Blue

Blue is a color of many moods. The color of the sea and sky, blue can have a tranquil, calming effect. Picture gentle aqua-colored waves lapping a sandy shore or the dusky cerulean blue of the sky at twilight. In its more dynamic shades, blue presents itself in the bright azure of the semiprecious stone, lapis lazuli, and in the glowing green-blue of polished turquoise. Blue can be energizing, even "electric." It is anything but predictable. Once in a "blue moon," it can catch you off guard, enticing you with its mottled flow of layered color as in a midnight sky. Blue can be as soft and sweet as a morning-glory, as brilliant as a peacock's breast, or as innocent as the blue of a robin's egg. Blue can play it as cool and smooth as slate, come on as powerfully as steel, or lay back as soft and cozy as an old pair of jeans.

Blue mixes beautifully with most other colors and can be seen in all seasons. Pastel blues like those found in the gemstone aquamarine works well with pale pinks and delicate lemon yellows, evoking a springy sensibility. Deep-hyacinth blue with a hint of lavender is gorgeous with leafy greens and earthy browns. Navy is a year-round nautical classic and has a crisp summer feel when highlighted with white. Add red, and blue becomes sporty. For fall and winter, mix royal blue or periwinkle with burnt golds and reds. Turquoise and crimson are a knockout pair with an Asian flair. For strong contrast, play up a sky blue with chocolate brown.

Peacock

A PEACOCK IN FULL PLUMAGE IS AMONG THE MOST SPEC-
TACULAR SIGHTS IN THE WORLD. THE EXOTIC "PEACOCK"
BRACELET, FEATURING BEADS IN AQUA, TEAL, AMBER, COP-
PER, AND GOLD, IS A GLAMOROUS NINE-STRAND BRACELET
THAT CONJURES THE COMPELLING ALLURE OF IRIDESCENT
COLOR. "PEACOCK" ALSO BOASTS BEADS IN AN ASSORTMENT
OF SHAPES AND SIZES—FACETED ROUND BEADS, OVALS,
BICONES, SQUARES, AND DISCS. TEAL BEADS WITH COPPER
EDGES, AQUA-BLUE BEADS FRAMED BY SCALLOPED GOLD
CAPS, AND FACETED AMBER DISCS ADD TO THE SPECTRUM
OF COLOR. AS A PEACOCK SHOWS OFF ITS MAGNIFICENT
FEATHERS IN BRILLIANT COLOR, SO TOO DOES THIS ONE-OF-
A-KIND BRACELET.

materials

- 6 clear-glass ovals, amber, 6mm wide, 10mm long
- 7 iridescent round glass beads, aqua, 8mm dia.
- 20 faceted discs, amber, 6mm dia., 3mm thick
- 19 faceted round glass beads, aqua, 6mm dia.
- 22 faceted clear-glass ovals, aqua, 8mm wide, 12mm long
- 8 square flat glass beads, amber with copper edges, 1cm wide, 1.6cm long
- 19 square flat glass beads, teal with copper edges, 8mm wide, 11mm long
- 25 Austrian-crystal bicones, aqua, 6mm
- 32 barrel spacer beads, gold, 3mm wide, 4mm long
- 21 round spacer beads, gold, 5mm dia.
- 55 round spacer beads, gold, 4mm dia.
- 51 round spacer beads, gold, 3mm dia.
- 14 bead caps, gold, 9mm dia.
- 2 end bars for 3 strands, gold, 2.5cm long
- 6 clamshells, gold
- 1 jump ring, gold, 18 gauge, 4mm dia.
- 1 lobster clasp, gold, 1.5cm long
- 1 spool of nylon beading thread, in white, size FF
- Cyanoacrylate (instant glue) gel
- Masking tape

tools

- Ruler, scissors, 3 twisted-wire beading needles, 2 chain-nose pliers

techniques

- How to Use a Clamshell (See pg. 167.)
- How to Attach a Clamshell (See pg. 167.)
- How to Make a Single- and Double-Overhand Knot (See pg. 168.)

Peacock

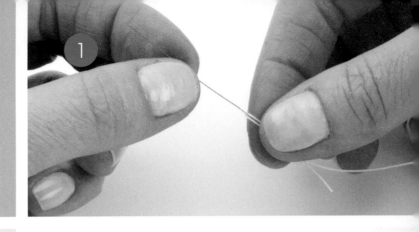

instructions

1.
Cut three 15-in. (38.1cm) lengths of beading thread. Thread a single length of thread into each needle.

2.
Thread all three needles through one clamshell.

3.
Pull the threads through the clamshell, and tie the ends together in a double-overhand knot, tying an additional single-overhand knot to ensure that the knot does not slip through the clamshell. Apply a drop of gel glue to the knot. Pull the knot into the clamshell, and trim off the thread ends. Close the clamshell.

4.
Set two of the threaded needles aside, and string beads on the third thread, referring to the Beading Layout, Group A (opposite). When the finished strand measures 7-in. (17.8cm), tape the end of the thread to your work surface.

5.
Repeat step 4 to bead the other two strands in Group A. Thread all three needles through another clamshell. Remove the needles. Repeat step 3.

6.
Attach the clamshell to an outside hole in one end bar using the chain-nose pliers.

7.
Attach the second clamshell to the corresponding hole in the second end bar using chain-nose pliers.

8.
Repeat steps 1–7 to bead and secure the beaded strands in Groups B and C as before.

9.
Open the jump ring. Thread it through the end of one end bar and the lobster clasp. Close the jump ring.

Beading Layout

Group A.

Group B.

Group C.

HELPFUL TIP
Creating a random mix of beaded
strands like those in "Peacock" provides
a great oppor-tunity to have fun!
You can play with colors, shapes,
and textures.

Azure Ice

The dangling beads on these dazzling hoop earrings seem to resemble icicles hanging from the eave of a Swiss ski chalet as the sun melts away the rooftop snow. Made from two silver hoops in graduating sizes, each "Azure Ice" earring combines crystal-clear iridescent beads, round beads in an icy blue, and bicones that call the deep bluish-green of the Arctic Ocean to mind. Sure to impress in any season, these wintry wonders are reminiscent of ice yet as unique as fresh-fallen snowflakes.

materials

- 92 Austrian-crystal beads:
  20 faceted iridescent, round, clear, 8mm dia.
  12 faceted, light blue, 4mm
  60 bicones, blue-green tourmaline, 4mm
- 30 headpins, silver, 20 gauge, 4cm long
- 32 jump rings, silver, 20 gauge, 4mm dia.
- 2 jump rings, silver, 20 gauge, 5mm dia.
- 2 square-wire hoops, silver, 20 gauge, 2.2cm dia.
- 2 square-wire hoops, silver, 16 gauge, 3.8cm dia.
- 1 pair leverback earrings, silver, 1cm wide, 1.4cm long

tools

- Wire cutters
- 2 chain-nose pliers
- Round-nose pliers

techniques

- How to Open and Close a Jump Ring (See pg. 166.)
- How to Make an Eye Loop (See pg. 170.)

Azure Ice

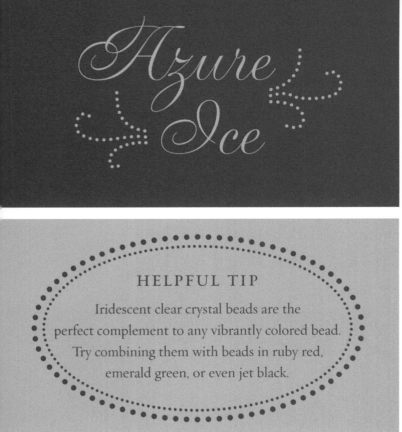

Beading Layout

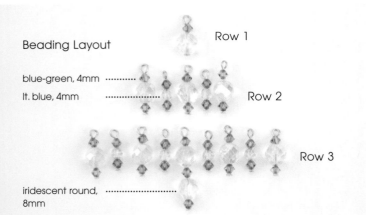

Row 1

blue-green, 4mm ··········

lt. blue, 4mm ················

Row 2

Row 3

iridescent round, ·····················
8mm

Beading Pattern

Row 1

Row 2

Row 3

instructions

1.
Use both pairs of chain-nose pliers to open one
4mm jump ring. Thread one end through the base
of one leverback earring. Close the jump ring.

2.
Use chain-nose pliers to open one 5mm jump ring.
Thread one end through the jump ring prepared in
step 1 and one large silver hoop.

3.
Thread on the small silver hoop. Close the 5mm
jump ring. Set the earring aside.

4.
Divide the iridescent round beads, the light-blue round
beads, and the blue-green bicone beads in half to make
two identical groups; set one group aside. Insert a headpin through one iridescent round bead and
one blue-green bicone to make one bead unit.

5.
Use the round-nose pliers to make an eye loop.
Following the Beading Layout (opposite), make 14
additional bead units as follows: bead seven headpins, each using two blue-green bicones and one iridescent round bead; bead six headpins, each using
two blue-green bicones and one light-blue round
bead; and bead one headpin using two iridescent
round beads and three blue-green bicones.

6.
Open one 4mm jump ring using the chain-nose pliers.
Thread one end through the eye loop on the bead
unit from step 4 and the base of the 5mm jump ring
from step 3. Close the jump ring to bead Row 1.

7.
Referring to Row 2 of the Beading Pattern, use a 4mm
jump ring to attach the beaded headpin in the center
of the row to the small hoop; then add two beaded
headpins to each side of the center bead.

8.
Referring to Row 3 of the Beading Pattern, use 4mm
jump rings to attach the beaded headpins to the large
hoop. Repeat steps 1–8 to make the second earring.

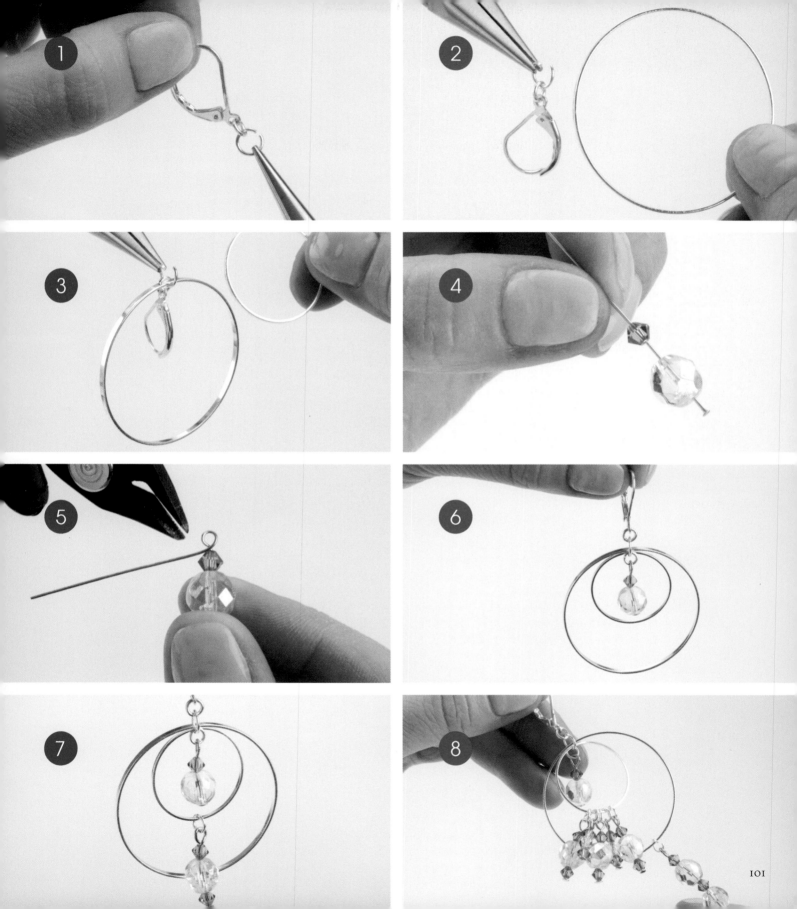

Ocean Breeze

"Even the upper end of the river," said the poet William Stafford, "believes in the ocean." The tranquil powder-blue color of this single-strand necklace fashioned from faceted nuggets suggests the foam on a cresting ocean wave. Another element of the seafaring sensibility of "Ocean Breeze" are the multicolored pearls in bubbly champagne, copper, bronze, white, pink, and shades of green that nestle snugly between small, round Austrian-crystal beads in light blue. Silver findings complete this sublime necklace summoning lasting images of surf and sea.

materials

- 18 faceted opaque nuggets, pale blue, 11mm wide, 18mm long, 14mm thick
- 17 freshwater pearls, 8mm dia., 6mm thick:
    6 champagne
    3 light green
    2 copper
    2 bronze
    2 white
    1 moss green
    1 pink
- 36 faceted Austrian-crystal round beads, light blue, 4mm dia.
- 2 clamshells, silver
- 2 crimp tubes, silver, size 2
- 1 spring ring, silver, 18mm dia.
- 1 ring, "figure-8" shape, silver
- Beading wire, 0.40mm dia.

tools

- Ruler
- Wire cutters
- Crimping pliers
- 2 chain-nose pliers

techniques

- How to Use a Crimp Tube/Bead (See pg. 166.)
- How to Use a Clamshell (See pg. 167.)
- How to Use a Clamshell to Cover a Crimp Tube/Bead (See pg. 167.)
- How to Attach a Clamshell (See pg. 167.)

Finished length: 23" (58.4cm)

Ocean Breeze

instructions

1.
Use wire cutters to cut a 35-in. (87.5cm) length of beading wire. Attach one end of the beading wire to the spring ring using a crimp tube and the crimping pliers. Then cover the crimp tube with a clamshell.

2.
Use chain-nose pliers to attach the clamshell to the spring ring. Trim away any excess beading wire.

3.
String one light-blue bead and one nugget onto the beading wire, hiding the cut end of the wire inside the beads. String on another light-blue bead and one pearl. Repeat this four-bead pattern 16 more times, randomly choosing a pearl in a different color each time. Finish by stringing on one light-blue bead, one nugget, and the last light-blue bead.

4.
Use crimping pliers, a crimp tube, and a clamshell to attach the "figure-8" ring to the end of the beading wire. Tuck the cut end of the beading wire into the last bead. Trim away any excess wire.

HELPFUL TIP

An alternative to using pearls in different colors to create this design is either to go monochromatic, using pearls in all the same color, or to choose two different colors, alternating the two.

Desert Sky

Although the Aztecs and Mesopotamians revered the varied shades of blue and the supposed healing powers of turquoise, this so-called Stone of the Desert is most commonly associated with the American Southwest. In "Desert Sky," a stunning opera-length necklace, polished stones in a classic turquoise blue are gracefully accented with sparkling sterling-silver beads and are connected to large silver jump rings to create a beaded chain. With its smooth, soothing stones in robin's egg blue and cyan, this decorative jewel all but transports you to a sun-drenched mesa or the breathtaking Enchantment.

materials

- 15 oval turquoise beads, 2.5cm wide, 3cm long
- 30 round beads, laser-finished sterling silver, 3mm dia.
- 15 jump rings, sterling silver, 14 gauge, 16mm dia.
- Silver wire, 18 gauge

tools

- Ruler
- Wire cutters
- 2 chain-nose pliers
- Round-nose pliers

techniques

- How to Open and Close a Jump Ring (See pg. 166.)
- How to Make a Wrapped-Wire Loop (See pg. 168.)

Finished length: 36" (91.4cm)

Desert Sky

1.
Use wire cutters to cut a 6-in. (15.2cm) length of wire. Make a wrapped-wire loop on one end.

2.
Rotate the wrapped-wire loop so that it is on the bottom. Insert the wire end through one silver bead and one turquoise bead.

3.
Thread a second silver bead onto the wire.

4.
Use the chain-nose and round-nose pliers to make a wrapped-wire loop above the silver bead added in step 3 to make one bead unit. Trim away any excess wire using the wire cutters.

5.
Repeat steps 1–4 with the remaining turquoise and silver beads to make an additional 14 bead units with wrapped-wire loops on each end. Use the chain-nose pliers to open one jump ring. Thread the jump ring through the wrapped-wire loops on two bead units. Close the jump ring.

6.
Open another jump ring. Thread it through one wrapped-wire loop from a third bead unit and the wrapped-wire loop on one end of the two units joined in step 5. Close the jump ring.

7.
Continue using the jump rings to join the bead units together to make a chain.

8.
Bring the two ends of the chain together. Use the chain-nose pliers to open the last jump ring, and thread it through the two wrapped-wire loops. Close the jump ring.

HELPFUL TIP

By incorporating jump rings into this design, you can control the length of the chain. Use fewer beads and jump rings to make this necklace shorter, or add more to make it long enough to double up around your neck!

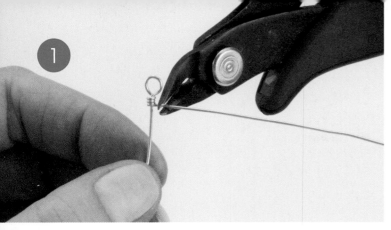

Watercolors

In China and Japan, watercolor painting has long been a beloved art form, and it lends its name to "Watercolors," a colorful, multistrand bracelet. A masterpiece of simplicity, the bracelet is fashioned from three strands of round aventurine beads in deep blue, square dyed shells in sky blue, and flat oval beads in light sapphire. Its true highlight resides in the elegant and ornate gold end bars, with their shimmering rhinestones in the dark-violet blue of indigo ink. A tasteful toggle clasp completes the appearance of this timeless objet d'art.

materials

- 38 opaque, round aventurine beads, blue, 6mm dia.
- 24 opaque, flat, square dyed-shell beads, light blue, 8mm
- 7 flat oval beads, light sapphire, 13mm wide, 18mm long
- 6 clamshells, gold
- 2 end bars for 3 strands, gold, studded with rhinestones
- 3 jump rings, gold, 18 gauge, 6mm dia.
- Toggle clasp, gold, 14mm dia.
- Cyanoacrylate (instant glue) gel
- Transite

tools

- Ruler
- Wire cutters
- 2 chain-nose pliers

techniques

- How to Open and Close a Jump Ring (See pg. 166.)
- How to Use a Clamshell (See pg. 167.)
- How to Attach a Clamshell (See pg. 167.)
- How to Make a Single- and Double-Overhand Knot (See pg. 168.)

Watercolors

instructions

1.
Use wire cutters to cut three 15-in. (38.1cm) lengths of transite. Set two lengths aside. Attach the end of one length to a clamshell. Use the other end of the strand to thread on three opaque, round aventurine beads.

2.
Continue to string on the beads in a pattern, referring to the photo or as desired. Attach the end of the beaded strand to a clamshell. Repeat step 1 to create the two remaining strands of beads.

3.
Attach the clamshell from one strand of beads to an outside hole in one end bar using the chain-nose pliers.

4.
Attach the clamshell at the opposite end of the strand to the corresponding hole in the second end bar using chain-nose pliers.

5.
Repeat steps 3–4 to attach the remaining two strands of beads to the end bars.

6.
Use a jump ring to join the loop on the end bar and the hoop section of the toggle clasp together. Join two jump rings together using pliers. At the opposite end of the bracelet, attach one jump ring to the end bar and the other jump ring to the bar section of the toggle clasp.

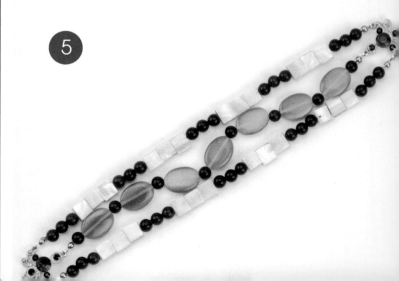

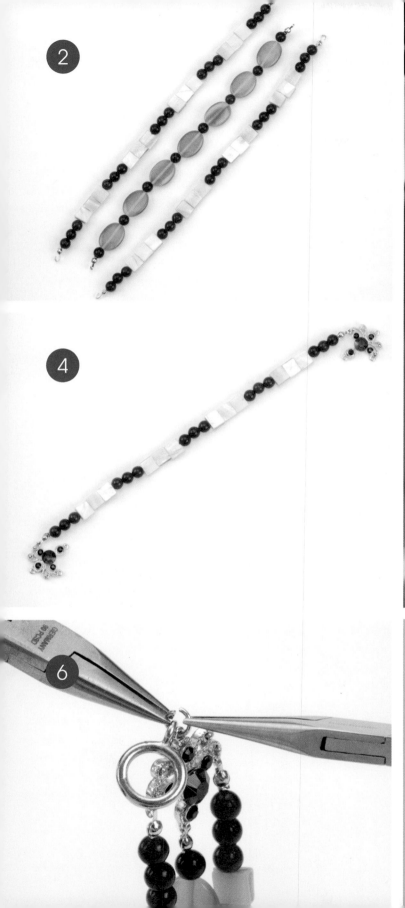

2

4

6

Starry Night

Vincent van Gogh's painting, *Starry Night*, is one of the most admired and enduring images in the world—its bright swirling "rockets" of burning yellow swirling against a deep-blue sky. The color of that masterwork's star-filled night also features prominently in this extravagant necklace in four shades of blue. In our "Starry night," fashioned from four separate, multistrand parts, seed beads in Persian blue and periwinkle combine with bugle beads in indigo and lavender blue. Each shade of blue reflects the light in a different way, effectively displaying even more subtle but captivating color variations. Modern-style sterling-silver findings and a spring-ring clasp add the final "brush strokes" to this shimmering masterwork in blue.

materials

- 1 hank crystal bugle beads, indigo, 2mm dia., 4mm long
- 1 hank crystal bugle beads, lavender blue, 2mm dia., 10mm long
- 1 hank seed beads, Persian blue, size 11
- 1 hank seed beads, periwinkle, size 11
- 184 silver-lined crystal seed beads, clear, size 6
- 8 bead caps, silver, 8mm dia., 16mm long
- 80 crimp tubes, silver, size 2
- 2 jump rings, silver, 7mm dia.
- 1 spring ring, silver, 18mm dia.
- 1 end ring in "figure-8" shape, silver
- Knot-tying beading wire, 0.019 in dia. (such as Soft Flex)

tools

- Ruler
- Wire cutters
- Crimping pliers
- 2 chain-nose pliers

techniques

- How to Open and Close a Jump Ring (See pg. 166.)
- How to Use a Crimp Tube/Bead (See pg. 166.)
- How to Make a Single- and Double-Overhand Knot (See pg. 168.)

Finished length: 22" (55.9cm)

Starry Night

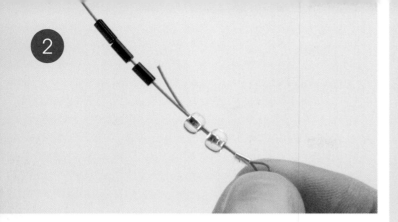

instructions

1.

Use wire cutters to cut nine 26-in. (66.0cm) lengths of beading wire. Use a crimp tube and crimping pliers to secure a small wire loop at the end of one length.

2.

Thread on two clear seed beads, hiding the cut end of the wire inside the beads. Then thread on 17 in. (43.2cm) of indigo bugle beads. Finish the strand by threading on another two clear seed beads.

3.

Thread a crimp tube onto the end of the strand, and use the crimping pliers to secure it, creating a loop as in step 1. Tuck the cut end of the beading wire into the last beads. Trim away any excess wire.

4.

Repeat steps 1–3 to bead the remaining eight lengths of wire with indigo bugle beads.

5.

Cut two 8-in. (20.3cm) lengths of beading wire. Thread one length through the looped ends of all nine beaded strands in indigo, centering the loops at the wire's mid-point. Tie two single-overhand knots to gather the strands.

6.

Thread the wire ends through one bead cap. Slide the cap down to cover the knots created in step 5.

7.

Gather the two wire ends together, and thread on five clear seed beads. Thread on a crimp tube, and attach the wire to the jump ring using crimping pliers. Tuck the wire end into the last beads, and trim off the excess wire. Repeat steps 5–7 to secure the opposite ends of the strands to the remaining jump ring.

8.

Repeat steps 1–7 to create three more groups of nine beaded strands using the remaining bead colors.

9.

Thread the end loop of each group of strands onto one of the jump rings used in step 7. Thread the end loop of each group of strands at the opposite end onto the other jump ring.

10.

Attach the "figure-8" ring to the jump ring on one end using pliers.

11.

Attach the spring ring to the jump ring on the opposite end of the strands using pliers.

117

Violet

VIOLET IS THE COLOR OF THE SPIRITUAL, THE SACRED, AND THE MYSTERIOUS. THE OPPOSITES OF HOT RED AND COOL BLUE, THIS INTRIGUING COLOR CALMS AND EXCITES AT THE SAME TIME: THINK OF THE SWEET, DEEP, PINKER TONES OF RARE VIOLET ORCHIDS, THE HAZY BUT BRILLIANT BLUE-VIOLET OF AN ARMFUL OF FRESHLY CUT LAVENDER, AND THE SENSUAL INDIGO OF A CLUSTER OF CONCORD GRAPES. VIOLET HAS A SPECIAL PLACE IN NATURE, OCCURRING RARELY BUT IN EYE-CATCHING WAYS THAT MAKE THE COLOR MORE VALUED AND REMARKABLE. VIOLET-HUED FLOWERS ARE OFTEN DELICATE AND CONSIDERED PRECIOUS; THE VELVETY DARK-PURPLE AFRICAN VIOLET IS A GOOD EXAMPLE. A PALE-VIOLET COLOR OFTEN TURNS UP AT THE SHORE, LENDING ITS DELICATE BEAUTY TO CLAMSHELLS AND SNAIL SHELLS. PRESENT IN A TRUE VIOLET SUNSET, THE SKY APPEARS LIT WITH SWIRLING PINKY MAUVES AND DUSKY AMETHYSTS. PURPLE HAS TRADITIONALLY BEEN ASSOCIATED WITH ROYALTY AND NOBILITY, AND HAS BEEN THE COLOR SYMBOLLIC OF WEALTH AND LUXURY IN MANY CULTURES. LEGEND HAS IT THAT CLEOPATRA HAD 20,000 SNAILS SOAKED FOR 10 DAYS TO OBTAIN ONE OUNCE OF PURPLE DYE FOR HER ROYAL ROBES!

VIOLET CAN MIX WITH BOTH COOL AND WARM COLORS. THE COLOR OF AN IRIS PAIRED WITH YELLOW IS A STRIKING COMBINATION. REDDER SHADES OF VIOLET BRING OUT THE BEAUTY OF REDS AND PINKS, AND FUCHSIA CAN REALLY "POP" WHEN COMBINED WITH A DEEP RED-ORANGE. PURPLE AND GREEN CAN BE ROMANTIC—PICTURE A NOSEGAY OF VIOLETS. ADDING A DASH OF YELLOW CAPTURES THE COLORS OF A VELVETY PANSY. THE LIGHT PURPLES OF LILACS AND LAVENDERS MINGLE BEAUTIFULLY WITH PALE SEA GREENS; AQUAS; SOFT, BUTTERY YELLOWS; AND PASTEL PINKS, EVOKING AN AURA OF ROMANTIC NOSTALGIA FOR BYGONE VICTORIAN DAYS.

Plum Wine

IMAGINE SAVORING THE TASTE OF RASPBERRIES IN A PLAYFUL PINOT NOIR OR THE PLUM FLAVOR OF A FINE CABERNET. AN INTOXICATING CONCOCTION FOR SOPHISTICATES, AS WELL AS THOSE WITH SLIGHTLY SIMPLER TASTES, "PLUM WINE" IS A MULTISTRAND NECKLACE WITH VICTORIAN TOUCHES FASHIONED FROM A COMBINATION OF CZECH CUT-CRYSTAL BEADS, SEED BEADS, AND PEARLS IN, FITTINGLY, THE COLORS PLUM AND WINE. OF PARTICULAR NOTE ARE THE DECORATIVE RHINESTONE MEDALLIONS THAT ACCENT THE RICH SWATH OF BEADED STRANDS THAT MAKE UP THE CENTRAL PART OF THE NECKLACE. HARVESTED FROM A PAIR OF EARRINGS AND REPURPOSED TO SERVE AS DECORATIVE END BARS, EACH MEDALLION HAS A LARGE PLUM-COLORED, FACETED AMETHYST SET IN AN OVAL FRAME IN STEEL-BLUE ENAMEL. ACCENTING EACH MEDALLION IS A MAJESTIC CROWN AND A RHINESTONE-STUDDED BOW, ADDING TO THE ELEGANT SENSE OF VICTORIANA.

materials

- 21 faceted, round metallic Czech cut-crystal beads, plum, 8mm dia.
- 60 faceted, round metallic Czech cut-crystal beads, plum, 4mm dia.
- 18 Austrian-crystal bicones, lavender, 4mm
- 36 seed beads, gold, size 11
- 1 hank seed beads, plum, size 11
- 42 glass pearls, wine, 6mm dia.
- 2 medallions, each with crown and bow, gold, with faceted amethyst in steel-blue setting, 1–2cm wide, 4mm long
- 26 crimp tubes, gold, size 2
- 2 jump rings, gold, 18 gauge, 5mm dia.
- 3 jump rings, gold, 18 gauge, 6mm dia.
- Toggle clasp, gold, 1.6cm dia.
- Beading wire, 0.32mm dia.

tools

- Ruler
- Wire cutters
- Crimping pliers
- 2 chain-nose pliers

techniques

- How to Open and Close a Jump Ring (See pg. 166.)
- How to Use a Crimp Tube/Bead (See pg. 166.)

Finished length: 22" (55.9cm)

Plum Wine

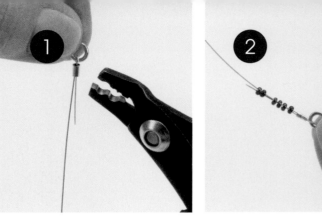

1

2

4

Beading Layout

A.

B.

C.

6

IMPORTANT TIP

Whenever you are attaching a crimp tube
or bead to a beaded strand, make certain that you
tuck the cut end of the beading wire into the last
beads, trimming away any excess wire
for a neat finish.

8

9

10

instructions

1.
Use wire cutters to cut 13 12-in. (30.5cm) lengths of beading wire. Attach one length to a 5mm jump ring using a crimp tube and crimping pliers.

2.
Thread on 7 in. (17.8cm) of plum seed beads to make one strand A, hiding the cut end of the wire inside the beads.

3.
Use a crimp tube and crimping pliers to attach a 5mm jump ring to the wire's end. Tuck the cut wire end into the last bead, and trim away the excess. Referring to the Beading Layout (opposite), repeat to bead seven more strand As, attaching the ends to the rings used here and in step 1.

4.
Repeat steps 1–3 to make two 7-in. (17.8cm) strand Bs using 4mm plum beads in the following pattern: thread on one gold seed bead, one bicone, one gold seed bead, and five 4mm plum beads; repeat this eight-bead pattern five more times, ending with one gold seed bead, one bicone, and one gold seed bead. Then repeat steps 1–3 to make one 7-in. (17.8cm) strand C using 8mm plum beads. Attach the strands to the same jump rings used in steps 1 and 3.

5.
Thread an open 6mm jump ring around the center of the bow on one medallion and through the 5mm jump ring at one end of the beaded strands. Close the jump ring.

6.
Repeat step 5 to attach the bow side of the second medallion to the opposite end of the beaded strands.

7.
At the crown end of one medallion, attach one strand of beading wire using a crimp tube and crimping pliers.

8.
Thread on one gold seed bead, one bicone, one gold seed bead, 21 pearls, one gold seed bead, one bicone, and one gold seed bead.

9.
Use a crimp tube and crimping pliers to attach a 6mm jump ring to the end of the beading wire.

10.
Use the jump ring attached in step 9 to attach the bar section of the toggle clasp to the jump ring.

11.
Repeat steps 7–8 to bead the second wire. Then attach the clasp's hoop section to the end with a crimp tube.

Wild Orchid

ORCHIDS, KNOWN FOR THEIR RICHLY COLORED BLOSSOMS, INSPIRE THIS ONE-OF-A-KIND NAMESAKE. BOTH A BROOCH AND A PENDANT FOR A NECKLACE, "WILD ORCHID" HAS FACETED DISCS IN AUBERGINE, WHICH ARE CLUSTERED TOGETHER TO CREATE A LARGE ORCHID "FLOWER." A SPRAY OF DELICATE BLUE FLOWERS MADE FROM BICONES AND ROUND BEADS SPRINGS UP BESIDE IT, ALONG WITH SMALL BUDS AND FRESH-GREEN LEAVES ALSO FASHIONED FROM SPARKLING BEADS. THIS DELICATE BOUQUET OF BEADED FLOWERS IS SECURED TO AN ORNATE GOLD PIN, BUT IT CAN ALSO BE SUSPENDED FROM A GOLD CHAIN, GIVING THIS DESIGN STYLISH VERSATILITY.

materials

- 18 faceted clear-glass discs, aubergine, 8mm dia., 3mm thick
- 4 flat clear-glass ovals, green, 8mm wide, 1.3cm long
- 2 faceted new-jade rondelles, light green, 5mm dia., 4mm long
- 3 faceted citrine briolettes, pale yellow, 8mm dia., 1.8cm long
- 1 round clear-glass bead, variegated pink, 8mm dia.
- 7 Austrian-crystal bicones, blue-green tourmaline, 4mm
- 7 faceted Austrian-crystal round beads, light blue, 4mm dia.
- 1 oval pendant setting, gold, 3.2cm wide, 3.6cm long
- 1 pin back, gold, 2cm long
- 2 jump rings, gold, 20 gauge, 4mm dia.
- Gold wire, 24 gauge
- 24" (60.9cm) cable-link chain, gold, 18 gauge, round wire, 3mm dia.
- 2 lobster clasps, gold, 1.3cm long
- Metal file
- Five-minute two-part expoxy, cardboard, toothpick

tools

- Ruler, wire cutters, 2 chain-nose pliers, round-nose pliers, chain cutters

techniques

- How to Make the Beaded "Wild Orchid Bouquet" (See pg. 172.)
- How to Open and Close a Jump Ring (See pg. 166.)

Finished length: 18" (45.7cm)

Wild Orchid

HELPFUL TIP

Once you've got the beading techniques down to make the "Wild Orchid," you can make any kind of flower imaginable. Try making beaded flowers in shades of scarlet, goldenrod, or lavender!

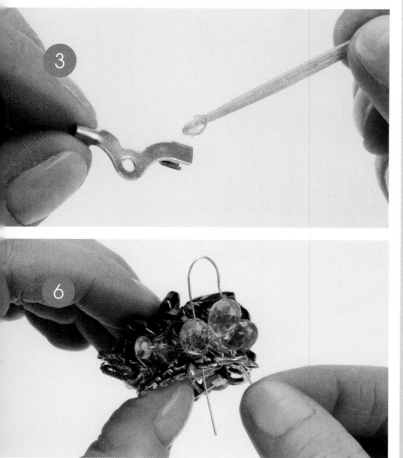

instructions

1.

Follow the directions, "How to Make the Beaded 'Wild Orchid Bouquet,'" on page 172 to make one purple flower, one blue floral spray, two green-leaf clusters, one yellow-briolette cluster, and one variegated-pink bud. Gather these elements together by their wire stems, and twist them together to secure the "bouquet."

2.

Bend the twisted-wire stem into two loops using the chain-nose and round-nose pliers. Set the bouquet aside.

3.

Mix two-part epoxy on scrap cardboard following the manufacturer's directions. Apply a dab of glue to the wrong side of the pin back using a toothpick.

4.

Center and press the pin back, glue side down, to the wrong side of the pendant setting. Let the glue cure.

5.

Use wire cutters to cut two 6-in. (15.2cm) lengths of gold wire. Bend the wires into U-shapes so that they resemble staples. Set them aside. Center the bouquet on the front side of the pendant setting.

6.

On one edge, thread the "legs" of the wire staple through the beaded flowers and the openings in the setting's filagree, exiting underneath the setting. Twist the wires together, tightening them against the back of the setting. Trim away the excess wire. Use the file to smooth the wires' cut ends. Repeat to secure the opposite side of the bouquet to the setting.

7.

Use chain cutters to cut a 16-in. (40.6cm) length of chain.

8.

Use the chain-nose pliers to open one jump ring. Thread it through the last link on one end of the chain and one lobster clasp. Close the jump ring. Repeat this step on the opposite end of the chain using the remaining jump ring and lobster clasp.

9.

Attach the lobster clasps to the openings in the filagree at the edge of the pendant setting to make a necklace.

Purple Reign

HISTORICALLY SPEAKING, THE COLORS PURPLE AND GOLD HAVE LONG BEEN ASSOCIATED WITH ROYALTY AND GREAT POWER. ROME, EGYPT, AND PERSIA USED THESE COLORS AS THE IMPERIAL STANDARD, AND IT IS BELIEVED THAT CLEOPATRA HERSELF FAVORED THE COLOR PURPLE. WITH THE REGAL "PURPLE REIGN," HISTORY REPEATS ITSELF. THE SINGLE-STRAND NECKLACE IS COMPOSED OF POLISHED TABLET-SHAPED BEADS IN SATURATED PURPLE SEPARATED BY FACETED ROUND BEADS IN BRILLIANT GOLD. EVER ELEGANT, THE ARISTOCRATIC "PURPLE REIGN" IS FINISHED WITH A CLASSIC GOLD CLASP, ADDING A FINAL "ROYAL TOUCH."

materials

- 27 rectangular flat glass beads, purple, 1cm wide, 1.5cm long
- 28 faceted round Czech cut-crystal beads, gold, 4mm dia.
- 2 clamshells, gold
- 1 jump ring, gold, 18 gauge, 6mm dia.
- 1 lobster clasp, gold, 1.4cm long
- 1 spool of nylon beading thread, cream, size FF
- Cyanoacrylate (instant glue) gel

tools

- Ruler
- Scissors
- 1 twisted-wire beading needle
- 2 chain-nose pliers

techniques

- How to Use a Clamshell (See pg. 167.)
- How to Attach a Clamshell (See pg. 167.)
- How to Make a Single- and Double-Overhand Knot (See pg. 168.)

Finished length 21" (53.3cm)

Purple Reign

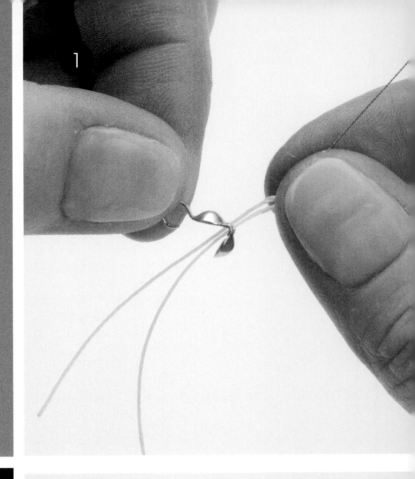

1

instructions

1.
Cut one 30-in. (76.2cm) length of beading thread. Attach a clamshell to the end of the thread opposite the needle.

2.
Insert the needle through one gold bead, and slide it down toward the clamshell.

3.
Thread on one purple bead followed by another gold bead. Continue to thread on beads, alternating the purple and gold beads until all the beads are used.

4.
Attach a clamshell to the end of the beaded thread after the last gold bead.

5.
Attach the jump ring to one clamshell.

6.
Attach the lobster clasp to the remaining clamshell.

4

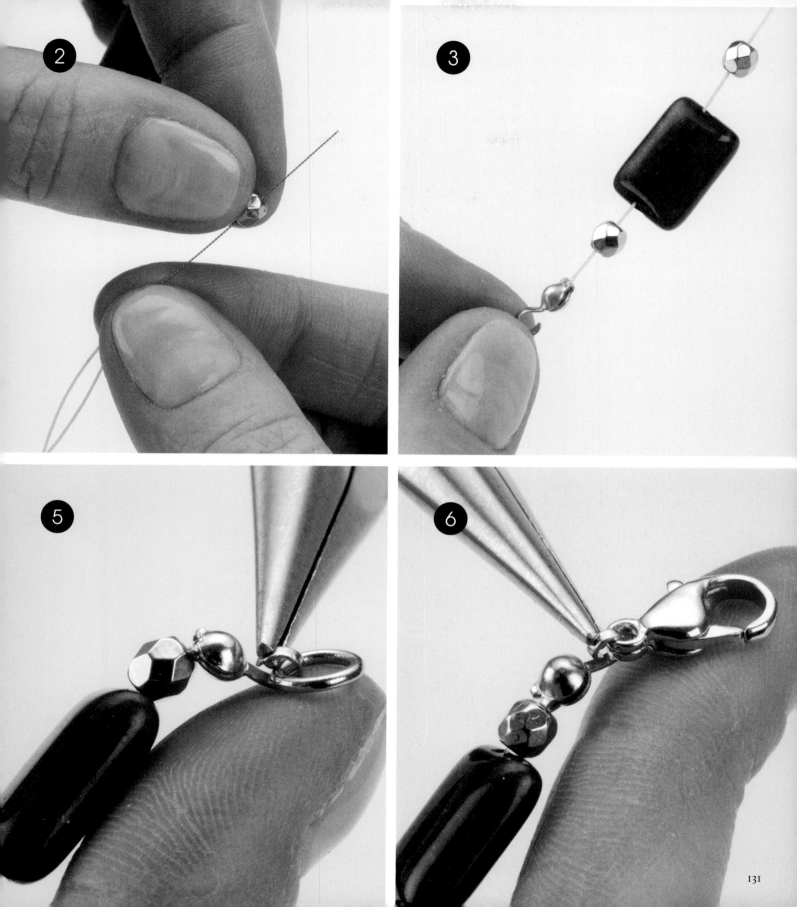

Peel Me a Grape

In the 1933 comedy *I'm No Angel*, legendary comedienne Mae West turned to her maid and uttered the classic line, "Beulah, peel me a grape." This memorable bit of dialogue inspired these playful drop earrings in light and dark amethyst, which strike a rather serious pose at first, but on closer inspection, resemble a cluster of grapes picked right off the vine. In "Peel Me a Grape," pale-green beads shaped like leaves and purple, faceted rondelles are suspended from a gold chain, which leads the eye to a faceted amethyst. A small but elegant fan is embossed onto the gold earrings, adding a bit of grandeur to this lighthearted creation.

materials

- 12 Austrian-crystal rondelles, amethyst, 6mm dia., 4mm long
- 12 Austrian-crystal rondelles, light amethyst, 6mm dia., 4mm long
- 2 faceted amethyst ovals, 1cm wide, 1.4cm long
- 8 glass leaf beads, light green, 9mm wide, 10mm long, 2mm thick
- Cable-link chain, gold, 24-gauge round wire, 2mm wide, 2mm long
- 22 headpins, gold, 3cm long
- 4 jump rings, gold, 22 gauge, 4mm dia.
- 8 jump rings, gold, 22 gauge, 5mm dia.
- Gold wire, 22 gauge
- 1 pair leverback earrings, brushed gold, 1cm wide, 1.4cm long

tools

- Ruler
- Wire cutters
- 2 chain-nose pliers
- Round-nose pliers

techniques

- How to Open and Close a Jump Ring (See pg. 166.)
- How to Make an Eye Loop (See pg.170.)
- How to Make an Eye Loop at Both Ends (See pg. 170.)
- How to Open and Close an Eye Loop (See pg. 169.)

Peel Me a Grape

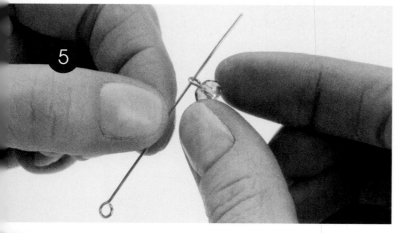

instructions

1.

Divide each type of bead into two halves; move one set of halves aside. Insert one headpin through an amethyst rondelle. Make an eye loop.

2.

Repeat step 1 to make eye loops on four more amethyst rondelles and six light-amethyst rondelles. Set them aside. Measure and cut a 2-in.(5.0cm) length of gold wire. Thread on the last amethyst rondelle, and make an eye loop on both ends.

3.

Thread an open 4mm jump ring through the base of one earring and the amethyst rondelle with eye loops. Close the jump ring.

4.

Cut a 1-in. (2.5cm) length of chain. Then open the second eye loop on the amethyst rondelle. Thread on the last link of the 1-in. (2.5cm) length of chain. Close the eye loop.

5.

Cut a 4-in. (10.2cm) length of gold wire. Make an eye loop on one end. Thread the other end through the eye loop on one light-amethyst rondelle. Let the bead slide down to the base of the wire just above the eye loop.

6.

Thread on one amethyst rondelle and a light-amethyst rondelle, letting the beads slide down the wire. Repeat four more times, alternating the two bead colors.

7.

Make an eye loop just above the top bead on the cluster of beads.

8.

Use the chain-nose pliers to open the eye loop made in step 7, and thread it through the last link on the free end of the chain. Close the eye loop.

9.

Cut a 4-in. (10.2cm) length of wire. Thread on one amethyst oval bead. Make an eye loop on both ends. Use the chain-nose pliers to open one eye loop on the bead, and thread it though the eye loop at the bottom of the beaded cluster. Close the eye loop.

10.

Use a 5mm jump ring to attach one green leaf to the eye loop on the top of the beaded cluster.

11.

Attach three more leaves to the top of the cluster. Repeat steps 1–11 to make the second earring.

African Violet

Going on safari but don't have anything fun to wear? This flirty charm bracelet incorporates beads with an exotic animal print along with shimmering glass discs in mauve, faceted round crystals in violet, and short, cylindrical cane beads in violet and red. "African Violet" makes clever use of a length of ball chain (replete with a key-chain style closure), which provides a sturdy, if witty, foundation for the beads that hang jauntily below.

materials

- 7 clear-glass discs with metallic interiors, mauve, 2.8cm wide, 6mm thick
- 7 faceted round clear-glass beads, violet, 12mm dia.
- 7 square flat glass beads with leopard pattern, mauve, 16mm
- 7 cane beads, purple-red-and-black, 7mm dia., 8mm long
- 28 Austrian-crystal bicones, light-pink, 4mm
- 14 faceted clear-glass rondelles, mauve, 6mm dia., 4mm long
- 14 silver-lined crystal seed beads, clear, size 11
- 28 headpins, silver, 6mm long
- 28 jump rings, silver, 16 gauge, 8mm dia.
- 12" (30.5cm) ball chain with clasp, silver, 7mm dia.

tools

- Ruler
- Wire cutters
- Chain cutters
- 2 chain-nose pliers
- Round-nose pliers

techniques

- How to Open and Close a Jump Ring (See pg. 166.)
- How to Make a Wrapped-Wire Loop (See pg. 168.)

African Violet

instructions

1.
Remove the clasp from the chain; set it aside. Then use chain cutters to cut off a 7-in. (17.8cm) length of chain.

2.
Reattach the clasp to one end of the chain.

3.
To make one bead unit A, insert one headpin through one bicone, one cane bead, and another bicone; make a wrapped-wire loop; repeat to make six more bead unit As.

4.
To make one bead unit B, insert one headpin through one rondelle, one violet bead, and another rondelle; make a wrapped-wire loop; repeat to make six more bead unit Bs. To make one bead unit C, insert one headpin through one seed bead, one leopard square bead, and another seed bead; make a wrapped-wire loop; repeat to make six more bead unit Cs. To make one bead unit D, insert one headpin through one bicone, one mauve disc, and another bicone; make a wrapped-wire loop; repeat to make six more bead unit Ds.

5.
Use the chain-nose pliers to open one jump ring. Thread the jump ring through the loop one bead unit D, the loop on one bead unit A, and the space between the first two balls on the chain. Close the jump ring.

6.
Thread an open jump ring through the loop on one bead unit C and the next open space between two balls on the chain. Close the jump ring. At the next open space, use a jump ring to attach one bead unit B. Repeat steps 5–6 six more times to attach the remaining bead units to the chain.

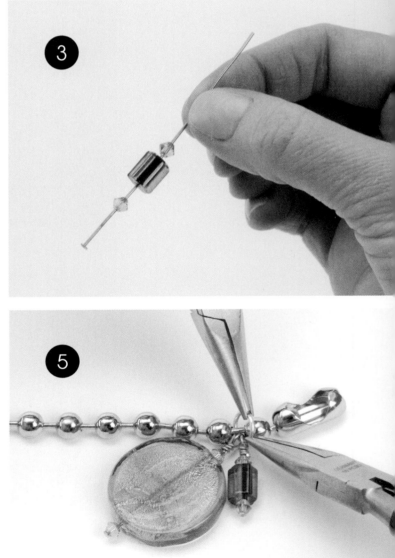

A.   B.   C.   D.

HELPFUL TIP

Chains are available in many colors, sizes, and styles. When choosing one, be sure to keep your design in mind. Remember that more beads add more weight, and a sturdy chain with thicker links will be required.

Lilac Festival

In the springtime, Rochester, New York; Spokane, Washington; and the Michigan island of Mackinac host glorious celebrations in honor of the cherished, fragrant flower, the lilac. Showing up in an exuberant array of shades—from pale and red violet and mauve, to pale purple, lilacs bloom for only a few weeks each year. Luckily, this multistrand necklace, "Lilac Festival" will last longer. An enduring classic, the polychromatic beads in lime, magenta, and lilac will continue to "bloom," making this festival a must-see attraction.

materials

- 196 faceted round quartz beads, magenta, 10mm dia.
- 9 faceted round new-jade beads, light green, 20mm dia.
- 29 faceted round quartz beads, lilac, 14mm dia.
- 41 opaque glass diamonds, lilac, 8mm wide, 14mm long
- 21 round dyed-turquoise beads, lime green, 10mm dia.
- 74 faceted new-jade rondelles, light green, 5mm dia., 4mm long
- 2 jump rings, silver, 14 gauge, 16mm dia.
- 14 crimp tubes, silver, size 2
- 1 lobster clasp, silver, 2.4cm long
- Beading wire, 0.40mm dia.

tools

- Ruler
- Wire cutters
- Crimping pliers
- 2 chain-nose pliers

techniques

- How to Open and Close a Jump Ring (See pg. 165.)
- How to Use a Crimp Tube/Bead (See pg. 166.)

Finished length: 24" (61.0cm)

Lilac Festival

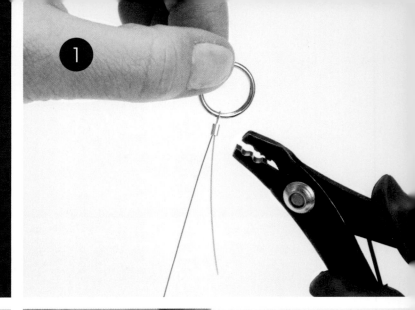

instructions

1.
Use the wire cutters to cut seven 30-in. (76.2cm) lengths of beading wire. Use a crimp tube and crimping pliers to attach a jump ring to the end of one length.

2.
Following the Beading Layout (opposite), choose one strand, and string on the corresponding beads.

3.
Thread a crimp tube onto the end of the strand, and attach the remaining jump ring using the crimping pliers.

4.
Using a crimp tube and the crimping pliers, attach another length of beading wire to the jump ring as in step 1. Thread on the beads, referring to the Beading Layout. Then, thread the end of the wire through a crimp tube and the jump ring attached in step 3, securing the crimp tube using crimping pliers. Bead and attach the remaining five strands as before.

5.
Open one jump ring at the ends of the strands using the chain-nose pliers. Thread on the lobster clasp. Close the jump ring. *Note: For the look of a soft "braid," gently twist the necklace before securing the clasp.*

Beading Layout

A.

B.

C.

D.

E.

F.

G.

Black and White

BLACK AND WHITE ARE OPPOSITES THAT TEAM UP TO MAKE A CLASSY AND CLASSIC PAIR. THIS DUO CALLS TO MIND THE TIMELESS ENSEMBLE OF BLACK-TIE AND TAILS OR THAT LITTLE BLACK DRESS WITH A STRAND OF PEARLS. BLACK-AND-WHITE CAN BE OLD-FASHIONED, LIKE YOUR GRANDMOTHER'S CAMEO BROOCH, OR RETRO, LIKE A PAIR OF SADDLE SHOES OR THE BLACK-AND-WHITE TILE FLOOR OF AN OLD-FASHIONED DRUGSTORE, COMPLETE WITH SODA FOUNTAIN. BLACK-AND-WHITE CREATES INSTANT GLAMOUR: PICTURE A SHINY BABY-GRAND PIANO. THE COMBINATION CAN BE FRISKY, LIKE A DALMATIAN, OR HEARTSTOPPING, LIKE A PAIR OF DICE TUMBLING ACROSS GREEN FELT. BLACK-AND-WHITE CAN COME ON BRAINY, LIKE A COMPOSITION NOTEBOOK FROM GRADE SCHOOL, OR ZANY, LIKE A PENGUIN SKITTERING ACROSS THE ICE. FROM DOMINOES TO OREOS, BLACK-AND-WHITE ARE YIN AND YANG, THE FRED AND GINGER OF COLOR SCHEMES.

NOT THAT BLACK AND WHITE CAN'T STAND ON THEIR OWN. BLACK, SYMBOLIC OF POWER AND SOPHISTICATION, COMMANDS INSTANT ATTENTION: THINK LONG BLACK LIMOS, SMOKY-BLACK EYELINER, AND A BLACK LEATHER BOMBER JACKET. WHITE CAN DO ALL THAT AND MORE—BUT WITH A TOUCH OF INNOCENCE: THINK THE WHITE FLASH OF DIAMONDS, A VASE OF PERFECT WHITE ROSES, AND CLEAN WHITE SHEETS HUNG ON THE LINE AND SNAPPING IN THE WIND.

WORKING TOGETHER, BLACK AND WHITE JAZZ UP THE PRIMARY COLORS RED, BLUE, AND YELLOW, AND ADD EXTRA ZIP TO SUCH BRIGHT JEWEL TONES AS TURQUOISE, DEEP VIOLET, EMERALD, AND MAGENTA. ALONE, BLACK CONTRASTS WELL WITH BRIGHT HUES AND MAKES THEM STAND OUT. COMBINED WITH STOPLIGHT RED, PARAKEET GREEN, OR HOT PINK, BLACK IS A POWERFUL EYE-GRABBER. WHITE CAN COZY UP TO PASTELS FOR A BABY-DOLL FEEL, BUT IT CAN ALSO PLAY UP HUES LIKE ORANGE AND COBALT BLUE.

After Midnight

This cosmopolitan creation features cubes of polished hematite, a mineral frequently found in tones of black, steel, or silver-gray, and used in jewelry for generations. In the modern, multistrand "After Midnight," reflective hematite cubes are strung together to create an elegant, high-gloss bracelet with a distinct metallic sheen. By catching the light at different angles, the cubes seem to change their color before your eyes. Hematite also possesses magnetic properties, which cause the individual strands of the bracelet to bond together to resemble a single, solid piece. A polished sterling-silver clasp adds a final flourish to this lustrous and literally "magnetic" creation.

materials

- 235 hematite cubes, 3mm sq.
- 10 crimp beads, sterling silver, size 1
- 1 hook-and-eye clasp, for 5 strands, sterling silver, 1.3cm wide, 1.5cm long
- Beading wire, 0.32mm dia.

tools

- Ruler
- Wire cutters
- Crimping pliers
- Chain-nose pliers

techniques

- How to Use a Crimp Tube/Bead (See pg. 166.)

After Midnight

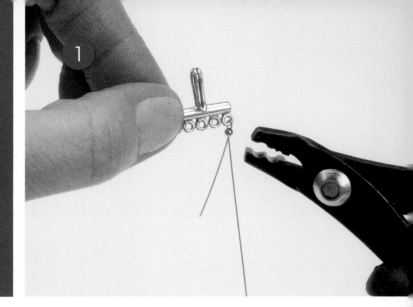

instructions

1.
Use wire cutters to cut five 10-in. (25.4cm) lengths of beading wire. Attach one wire strand to an outside hole in one half of the clasp using a crimp bead and crimping pliers.

2.
Thread on 47 beads, hiding the cut end of the wire inside the beads. The beaded strand should measure 6 in. (15.2cm) long.

3.
Use a crimp bead and the crimping pliers to attach the other end of the strand to the corresponding outside hole in the second half of the clasp. Tuck the wire end into the last beads.

4.
Position the bracelet as shown, ensuring that the clasps are parallel with one another. Repeat steps 1–2. As each new bead is strung onto the beading wire, it should line up with and be magnetically pulled by the cubes around it. Repeat step 3 to finish this strand.

5.
Repeat steps 1–4 to attach the remaining three strands of beads to the corresponding holes in both ends of the clasp.

6.
To fix an "unruly" cube that prevents the strands from bonding together and lying flat, pull the strands apart and rotate the cube on the strand. *Note: A different side can change the attraction to the cubes around it.*

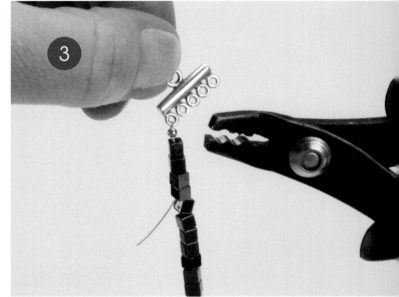

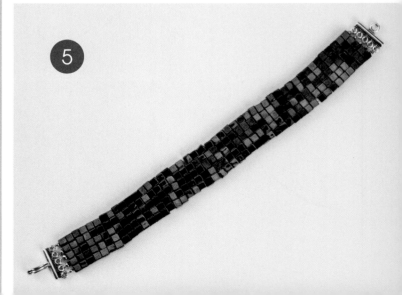

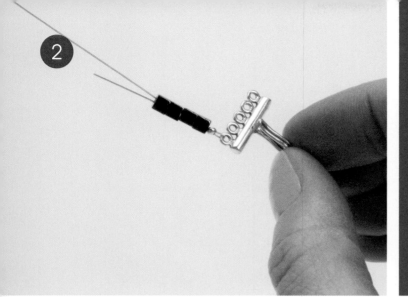

2

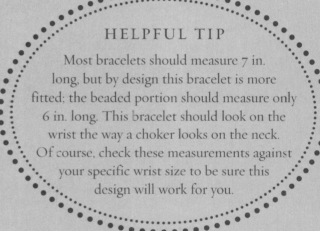

HELPFUL TIP

It is important to string the cubes and the beaded strands in a certain direction because hematite is magnetic. Be sure to check your work as you go to make sure that the cubes are attracting—and not repelling, the cubes around them to avoid compromising the finished look.

4

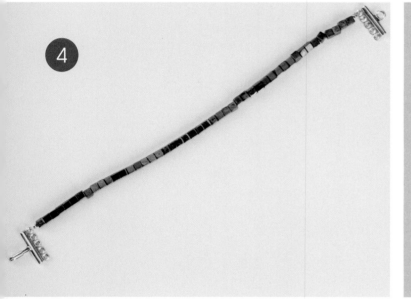

HELPFUL TIP

Most bracelets should measure 7 in. long, but by design this bracelet is more fitted; the beaded portion should measure only 6 in. long. This bracelet should look on the wrist the way a choker looks on the neck. Of course, check these measurements against your specific wrist size to be sure this design will work for you.

6

Sparkling Moonlight

Dangling from delicate silver chains, a sparkling array of crystals, pearls, and charms makes up "Sparkling Moonlight," a bracelet that conjures images of the full moon glowing in an inky-black sky. This alluring charm bracelet is constructed from five strands. It includes a narrow rhinestone chain and four sterling-silver chains with an eclectic assortment of shimmering charms that dazzle and dance like moonlight on the surface of a bay: rhinestone circle charms, faceted Austrian-crystal cubes, filigree balls in silver, crystal bicones, and large white pearls, with each pearl resembling a silvery moon in full glory.

materials

- 3 rhinestone circle charms, set in gold, 12mm dia.
- 3 glass pearls, white, 12mm dia.
- 3 Austrian-crystal bicones, clear, 6mm
- 3 filigree round beads, silver, 8mm dia.
- 3 seed beads, clear, silver lined, size 11
- 5 faceted Austrian-crystal cubes. clear, 8mm sq.
- 12" (30.5cm) rhinestone chain, silver setting, 2mm sq.
- 30" (76.2cm) cable-link chain, sterling silver, 22 gauge, 3mm-dia. links
- Silver-plated copper wire with matte finish, white, 24 gauge
- 2 round-end rhinestone chain end-connectors, silver, 3mm wide, 6mm long, 2mm thick
- 8 ball-tipped headpins, silver, 24 gauge, 4cm long
- 17 jump rings, silver, 22 gauge, 5mm dia.
- 3 jump rings, silver, 18 gauge, 6mm dia.
- 6 jump rings, silver, 18 gauge, 7mm dia.
- 1 spring ring, silver, 6mm dia.

tools

- Ruler, wire cutters, 2 chain-nose pliers, round-nose pliers

techniques

- How to Open and Close a Jump Ring (See pg. 166.)
- How to Make a Wrapped-Wire Loop (See pg. 168.)

Sparkling Moonlight

1

3

4

6

HELPFUL TIP

Experiment with the lengths of the chains so that they are not all of equal length. A ½-in. (12.7mm) or even a 1-in. (2.5cm) difference between the lengths will produce a bracelet with more interesting style.

8

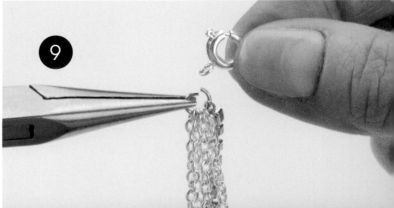

9

Beading Layout

A.

B.

C.

D.

E.

1.

Cut three 7-in. (17.8cm) lengths and one 4-in.(10.2cm) length of silver chain; set the lengths aside.

2.

Refer to the Beading Layout (opposite). Make strand A: cut three 6-in. (15.2cm) lengths of white wire. Make a wrapped-wire loop on each end of three pearls. Cut the 4-in. (10.2cm) length of chain into two ¾-in. (19.1mm) lengths and two 1¼-in. (3.2cm) lengths. For the center pearl, use 7mm jump rings to join two ¾-in. (19.1mm) lengths to one pearl. Then use a 7mm jump ring to join one 1¼-in. (3.1cm) length to each of the remaining pearls. Join the four segments together using 7mm jump rings: join the end loop on each of the pearls with one chain to a ¾-in. (19.1cm) length of chain.

3.

Make strand B: make wrapped-wire loops on both ends of all three crystal bicones; set two aside. Cut a 7-in. (17.8cm) length of chain into two pieces. Use 5mm jump rings to join one chain to each of the end loops on the bicone. Use a headpin to make a wrapped-wire loop on each of the five cubes. Use five 5mm jump rings to attach the cubes anywhere on the chain.

4.

Cut a 7-in. (17.8cm) length of rhinestone chain.

5.

Make strand C: set the last rhinestone on the chain inside one rhinestone chain end-connector. Use the chain-nose pliers to bend the prongs flush against the stone. Repeat at the opposite end of the rhinestone chain.

6.

Make strand D: cut 7 in. (17.8cm) of silver chain into three unequal lengths. Rejoin the sections with the two remaining bicones (set aside in step 3) using 5mm jump rings. Thread a headpin through one filigree silver ball and one seed bead; make a wrapped-wire loop. Repeat two more times. Attach the balls to the chain using 5mm jump rings. Trim excess chain so that strand D is 7 in. (17.8cm).

7.

Make strand E: use 5mm jump rings to attach the rhinestone circle charms on the remaining length of silver chain.

8.

Attach the ends on one side of the strands using a 6mm jump ring, and attach a 6mm jump ring to that jump ring.

9.

Attach the opposite ends of the strands to a 6mm jump ring, and thread on a spring-ring clasp.

"LUCK, BE A LADY" WROTE COMPOSER FRANK LOESSER IN THE CLASSIC STAGE MUSICAL *GUYS AND DOLLS*. A SHOWSTOPPER IN ITS OWN RIGHT, "LADY LUCK" IS A ONE-OF-A-KIND CHARM BRACELET CONSTRUCTED FROM A STURDY STERLING-SILVER CHAIN THAT SPORTS A DIVERSE ARRAY OF BLACK-AND-WHITE CHARMS FASHIONED FROM BLOWN GLASS AND CERAMIC BEADS. AMONG THESE ARE GLASS SQUARES WITH ZEBRA STRIPES, BLACK-AND-WHITE LADYBUGS, GIRAFFES WITH BLACK SPOTS, BLACK-AND-WHITE FLOWERS, AND BLACK RONDELLES WITH WHITE POLKA DOTS. WITH THE ADDITION OF LIME GREEN, AQUA, AND ORANGE BEADS TO CREATE A SURPRISING "POP" OF COLOR AND A SMART SILVER LOBSTER CLASP TO ROUND OUT THE LOOK—LUCKY LADY, YOU'VE HIT THE JACKPOT!

materials

- 6 round dyed-turquoise beads, lime green, 10mm dia.
- 4 square flat glass beads with zebra stripes, black-and-white, 16mm sq.
- 3 ceramic ladybug beads, black, white, and red, 10mm dia., 12mm long
- 2 clear round cane beads with black and white stripes, 14mm dia., 9mm thick
- 2 ceramic flower beads, white with black center, 2cm dia.
- 2 ceramic flower beads, black with white center, 2cm dia.
- 2 opaque glass giraffe beads, white with black spots, 20mm wide, 25mm long, 8mm thick
- 2 clear-glass rondelles with black opaque centers and white polka dots, 15mm dia., 12mm thick
- 2 opaque square flat glass beads, black with white stripes, 20mm sq.
- 1 clear square cane bead with black, white, and green stripes, 15mm sq., 8mm thick
- 1 ceramic Asian doll-head bead, 13mm wide, 20mm long, 12mm thick
- 1 ceramic Asian doll-head bead, 15mm wide, 18mm long, 10mm thick
- 1 ceramic stripe flower bead, black, white, and blue, 10mm dia., 8mm thick
- 1 ceramic stripe flower bead, black, white, and yellow, 10mm dia., 8mm thick
- 1 opaque glass cross, black-and-white stripes, 26mm wide, 44mm long, 4mm thick
- 12 faceted opaque round beads, aqua, 4mm dia.
- 30 opaque round beads, orange, 4mm dia.
- 12" (30.5cm) cable-link chain, sterling silver, with links 1cm dia.
- 30 headpins, silver, 6cm long
- 31 jump rings, silver, 18 gauge, 7mm dia.
- 1 jump ring, silver, 16 gauge, 8mm dia.
- 1 bail, silver
- 1 lobster clasp, silver, 14mm long
- Crystal cement

tools

- Ruler
- Wire cutters
- Chain cutters
- 2 chain-nose pliers,
- Round-nose pliers

techniques

- How to Open and Close a Jump Ring (See pg. 166.)
- How to Make a Wrapped-Wire Loop (See pg. 168.)

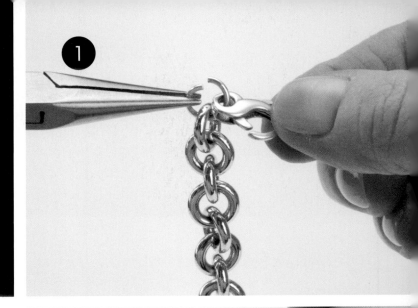

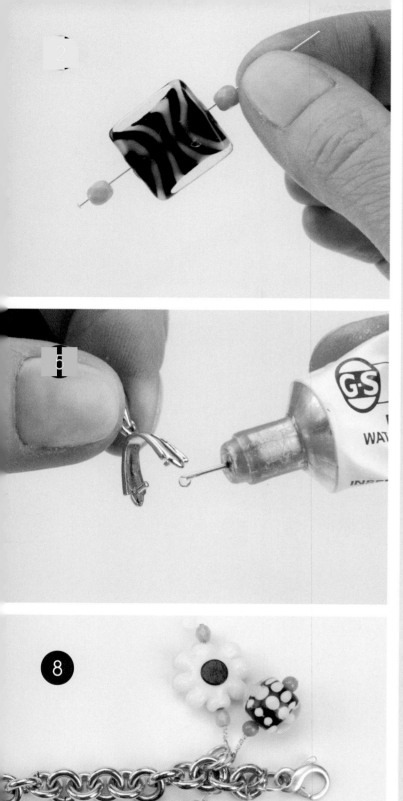

1.
Use chain cutters to cut a 7-in. (17.8cm) length of chain. Open an 8mm jump ring using the chain-nose pliers. Thread it through the lobster clasp and the last link on one end of the chain. Close the jump ring.

2.
Insert one headpin through one aqua bead, one square zebra-striped bead, and another aqua bead. Make a wrapped-wire loop. Set the bead unit aside.

3.
Lay out your beads on a flat surface. Referring to the photo, insert a headpin through the corresponding beads, and make a wrapped-wire loop. Set the finished bead units aside.

4.
To attach the bail to the cross charm, first test-fit the bail on the cross to ensure that it is wide enough to safely slip over the end of the cross. If it isn't, use the chain-nose pliers to adjust it.

5.
Add a drop of crystal cement to the pegs inside the bail.

6.
Slip the bail over the end of the cross, and insert the pegs into the hole. Use the chain-nose pliers to gently squeeze the sides of the bail together. Let the glue dry.

7.
Open a 7mm jump ring using the chain-nose pliers. Thread it through one bead unit and one link on the chain. Close the jump ring.

8.
Continue to attach the remaining 30 bead units in any order using the remaining 7mm jump rings.

Black ~ Tie Affair

Planning to attend an evening wedding, a smart dinner party, or perhaps opening night at the opera? This sublime necklace with sterling-silver accents is the ideal accessory. A sleek, chic stunner featuring a sheer black organdy ribbon with satin edges, the highlight of this "Black-Tie affair" is a cut-crystal pendant that catches and reflects the light, adding a dash of flash to the otherwise formal proceedings. Whether complementing a fabulous evening dress or "classing up" a slightly more casual ensemble, this dashing dazzler is truly an affair to remember.

materials

- 1 faceted Czech cut-crystal briolette, clear, 3.3cm dia., 4cm long
- ½ yd. (45.4cm) organdy ribbon with satin edge, black, ⅝" (15.8mm) wide
- Sterling-silver wire, 18 gauge
- 1 bail, sterling silver
- 2 round-end end-cap connectors, sterling silver
- 2 jump rings, silver, 18 gauge, 5mm dia.
- 1 hook-and-eye clasp, sterling silver
- Crystal cement
- Toothpicks

tools

- Ruler
- Wire cutters
- 2 chain-nose pliers
- Round-nose pliers
- Scissors

techniques

- How to Open and Close a Jump Ring (See pg. 166.)

Finished Size: 20" (50.8cm)

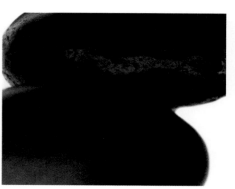

159

Black~Tie Affair

1.

Use wire cutters to cut a 10-in. (25.4cm) length of wire. Insert the wire through the crystal briolette so that 3 in. (7.6cm) of wire is on one side and the remaining length of wire is on the other. Bend up both wire ends.

2.

Use round-nose pliers to grip the short end of wire at its midpoint. Rotate the pliers away from the crystal briolette to form a loop directly over the tip of the bead.

3.

Use chain-nose pliers to grasp the loop. With the other hand, grasp the long wire. Bring it behind the loop and around to the front, trapping the wires at the base of the loop.

4.

Continue to wrap the long wire around the wire stem and the top of the crystal briolette. Finish on the backside. Trim away any excess wire.

5.

Use the chain-nose pliers to gently squeeze the cut-wire end flush against the briolette.

6.

Insert the peg inside the bail into the loop on the crystal briolette. Use the chain-nose pliers to squeeze the ends of the bail together. For extra security, place a drop of crystal cement on the inside where the end of the peg and the body of the bail meets. Let the glue dry.

7.

Use the scissors to cut an 18-in. (45.7cm) length of ribbon.

8.

Insert the end of the ribbon through the loop on the bail, and slide the crystal briolette to the ribbon's midpoint.

9.

At one end of the ribbon, tie a knot. Grasp the end of the ribbon using the pliers, and pull to make the knot as tight and as small as possible. Trim away the excess ribbon. Repeat on the opposite end of the ribbon.

10.

Apply crystal cement to one ribbon knot. Use a toothpick to push the knot into one end-cap connector. Let the glue dry. Repeat these steps to attach the second end-cap connector.

11.

Thread an open jump ring through one connector and the hook section of the clasp. Close the jump ring. Repeat this step to attach the remaining section of the clasp to the end-cap connector at oposite end of the ribbon.

Beading Basics

TOOLS • MATERIALS • TECHNIQUES

Beading Basics

THIS SECTION OF **THE COLOR BOOK OF BEADED JEWELRY** IS DESIGNED TO BE A HELPFUL, AT-YOUR-FINGERTIPS REFERENCE GUIDE TO THE BASICS OF JEWELRY-MAKING AS THEY APPLY TO THE BEAUTFUL DESIGNS INCLUDED IN "THE COLLECTION."

basic tools

The number of tools needed to accomplish the basic beading techniques is small, but each tool is designed to make a particular technique easier to do, thereby helping to ensure fine workmanship.

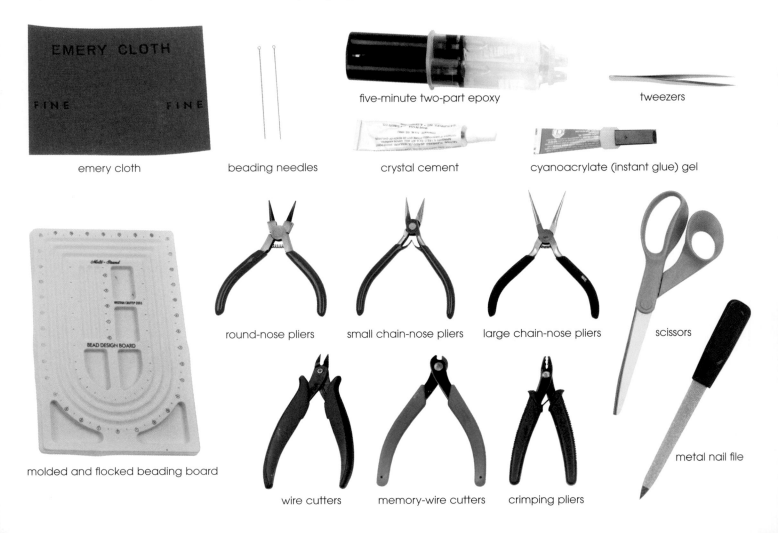

emery cloth

beading needles

five-minute two-part epoxy

tweezers

crystal cement

cyanoacrylate (instant glue) gel

molded and flocked beading board

round-nose pliers

small chain-nose pliers

large chain-nose pliers

scissors

wire cutters

memory-wire cutters

crimping pliers

metal nail file

basic materials

BEADS

Beads come in an infinite number of sizes, shapes, and materials. Here is a pretty array of beads that shows a few available styles.

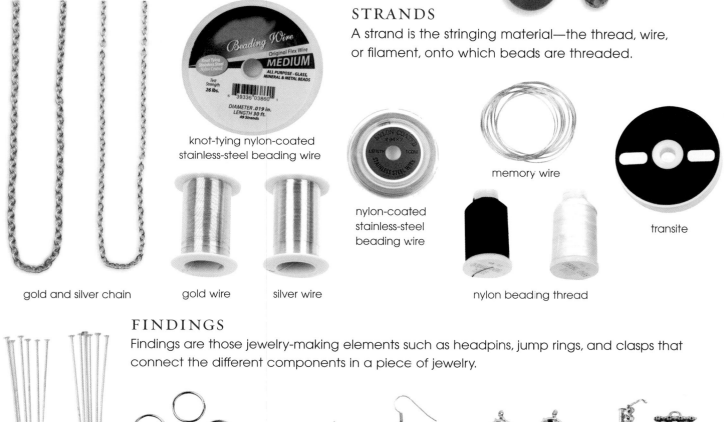

knot-tying nylon-coated
stainless-steel beading wire

gold and silver chain

gold wire

silver wire

STRANDS

A strand is the stringing material—the thread, wire, or filament, onto which beads are threaded.

nylon-coated
stainless-steel
beading wire

memory wire

transite

nylon beading thread

FINDINGS

Findings are those jewelry-making elements such as headpins, jump rings, and clasps that connect the different components in a piece of jewelry.

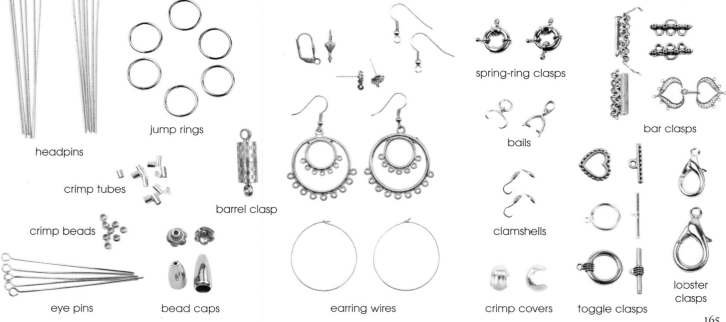

headpins

jump rings

crimp tubes

barrel clasp

crimp beads

eye pins

bead caps

earring wires

spring-ring clasps

bails

clamshells

crimp covers

bar clasps

toggle clasps

lobster
clasps

basic techniques

HOW TO USE A CRIMP TUBE/BEAD

Crimp tubes and crimp beads are used with crimping pliers to secure strand material to findings.

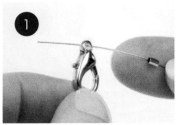

To attach a lobster clasp, thread a crimp tube and a lobster clasp onto beading wire.

Thread the end of the short wire back through the crimp tube.

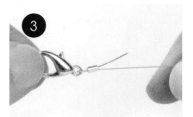

Hold the wires, and slide the crimp tube against the base of the clasp.

Place the crimp tube in the back, crescent portion of the crimping pliers, and press down. DETAIL: Make sure that one wire is in each channel of the crimp tube.

Place the crimp tube in the front portion of the crimping pliers, and press down to fold the crimp tube in half. DETAIL: The completed crimp tube should look like this when finished.

*TIP: Crimp tubes and crimp beads serve the same purpose, and they are attached using the same technique. It is important to choose a crimp tube or a crimp bead through which the strand(s) can snugly pass. Then follow the steps to attach it.

HOW TO OPEN/CLOSE A JUMP RING

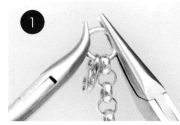

Use two pairs of pliers to grasp the closed jump ring on opposite sides as shown.

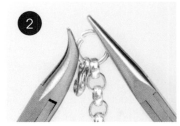

Rotate your wrists, moving one toward you and the other away to open the ring. Reverse the action to close the jump ring.

HOW TO USE A CRIMP COVER

Crimp covers resemble small hollow round beads, and are available in gold and silver. They are decorative elements used to conceal crimp tubes and crimp beads. They are very simple to use and are entirely optional; using them depends solely on the desired look you are going for.

After the crimp tube* is secured, grasp one crimp cover with the opening facing outward in the tips of the chain-nose pliers.

Position the crimp cover over the crimp tube and center it.

Squeeze the pliers using gentle and steady pressure until the edges of the crimp cover touch.

Check to ensure that there are no gaps or openings. The closed crimp cover should look like a small round bead, as shown.

* The technique detailed here can also be used to cover a crimp bead.

HOW TO USE A CLAMSHELL

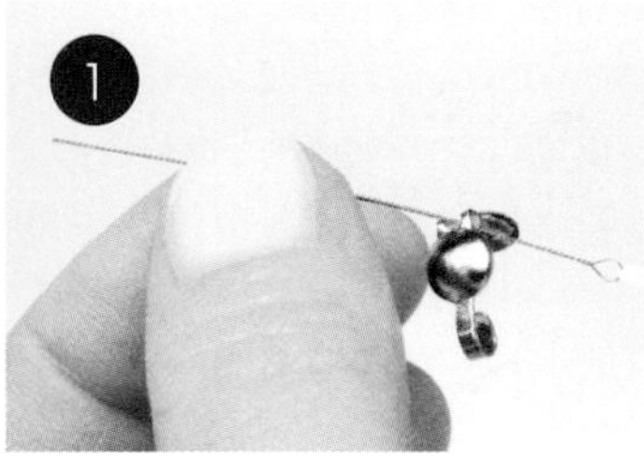

Double-thread a beading needle, and make a double-knot at the end of the thread. Insert the needle through the hole in the clamshell from the inside.

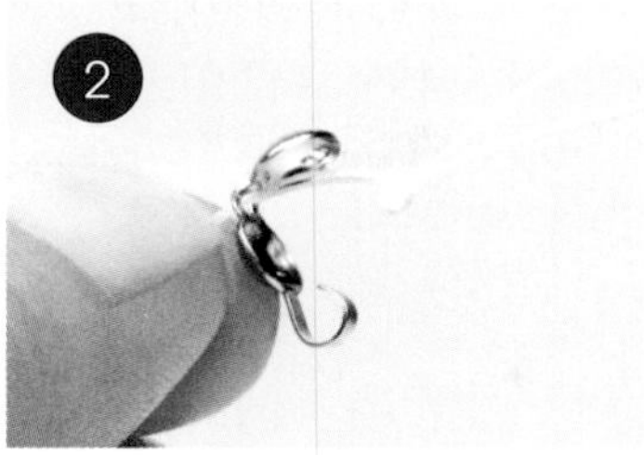

Pull the thread through the clamshell until the knot is about ½ in. (1.2cm) away from the clamshell.

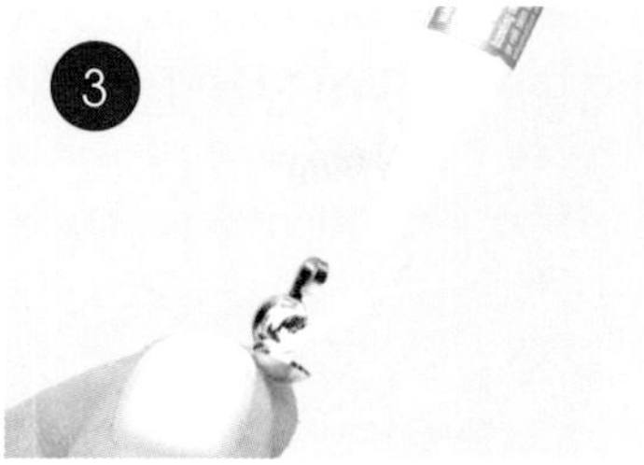

Cut the ends of the thread to nubs as shown. Place a drop of glue on the knot to secure it.

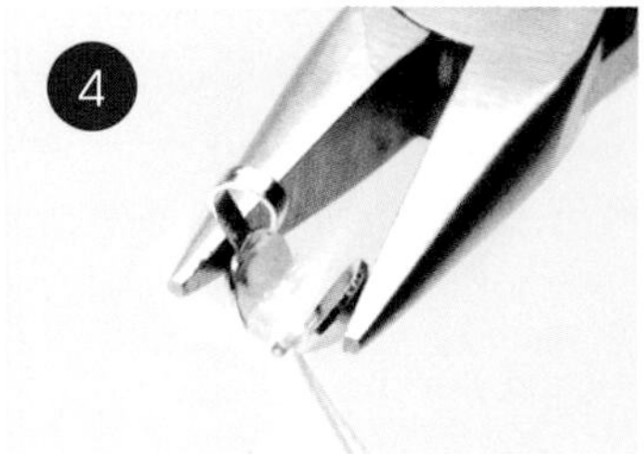

Pull the knot into the clamshell. Close the clamshell using the chain-nose pliers. Use the needle at the opposite end of the thread to string on beads.

HOW TO ATTACH A CLAMSHELL

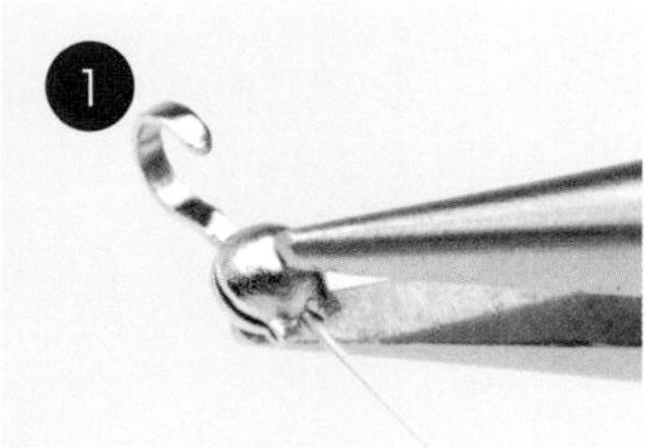

Use pliers to grasp the open halves of the clamshell. Slowly squeeze the halves together, trapping the knot inside.

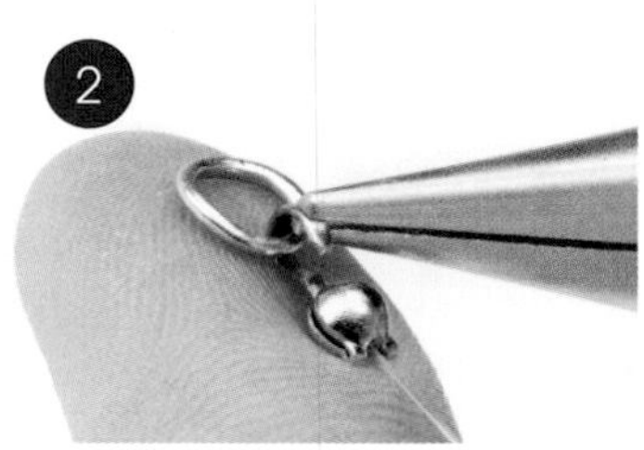

Place a jump ring in the clamshell's hook as shown. Grasp the front of the hook using the chain-nose pliers.

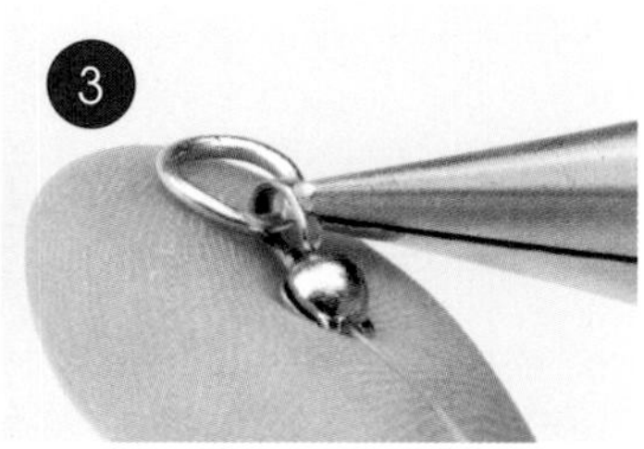

Roll the pliers toward you to bend the hook around the jump ring to secure it.

HOW TO USE A CLAMSHELL TO COVER A CRIMP TUBE/BEAD

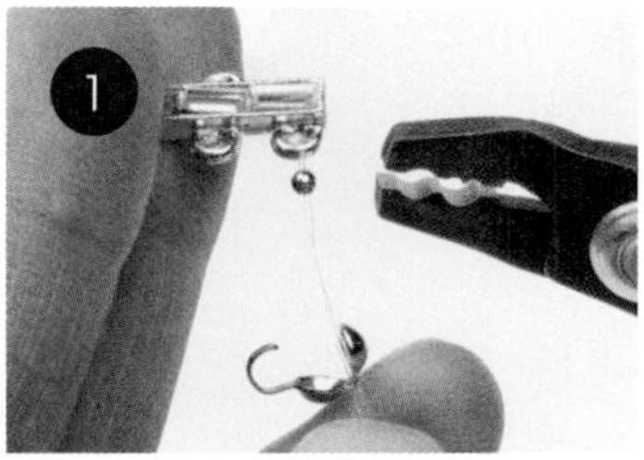

Thread the strand through a clamshell, a crimp bead*, and one hole in the bar clasp. Thread the end of the strand back through the crimp bead. Use the crescent-shaped portion of the crimping pliers to secure the crimp bead.

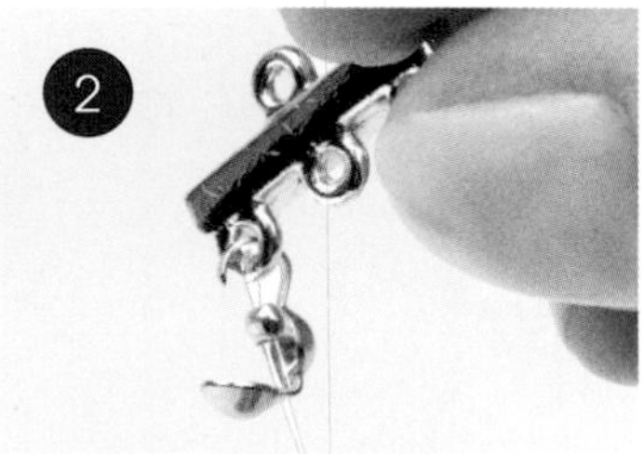

Slide the clamshell along the strand until the crimp bead is inside the clamshell and the hook on the clamshell is threaded through the hole in the bar clasp.

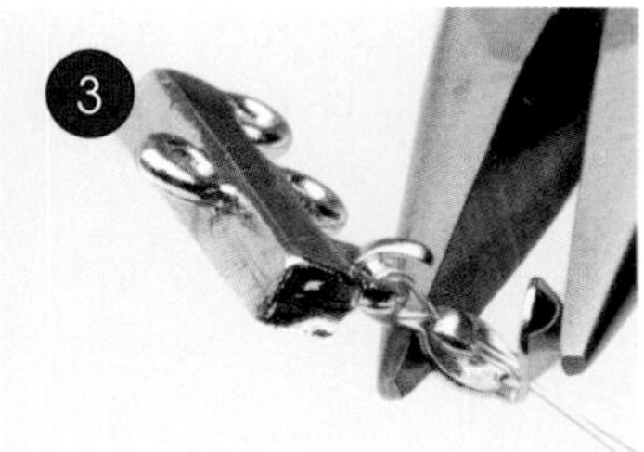

Use chain-nose pliers to close the clamshell, trapping the crimp bead inside.

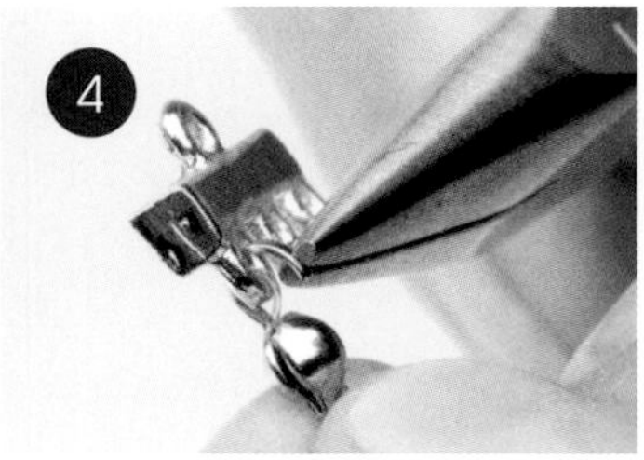

Use pliers to grasp the hook and roll it toward you to secure the clamshell to the barclasp, and to hide the strand at the same time.

* The technique detailed here can be used to cover a crimp tube and a crimp bead.

basic techniques (cont'd.)

HOW TO MAKE A WRAPPED-WIRE LOOP

Note: the following directions use cut-wire lengths to make wrapped-wire loops. If you are using one to make a wrapped-wire loop at each end of a bead, insert the wire into the bead, and make the first wrapped-wire loop; then use the wire at the opposite side of the bead to make a second loop. If you are using a headpin instead, insert the headpin into the bead, and use the wire that extends beyond the bead to make a wrapped-wire loop.

Cut a 6-in. (15.2cm) length of wire. Use chain-nose pliers to grasp the wire 2 in. (5.0cm) from one end. Turn the pliers away from you to bend the wire at a 90-deg. angle.

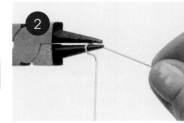

Grasp the wire 1/8 in. (3.0mm) from the bend using the round-nose pliers. Rotate the pliers toward the bend.

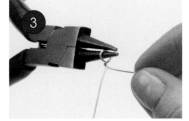

Use your fingers to wrap the wire around one jaw of the pliers, crossing the wire in front of the stem to make a loop, and wrapping the wire completely around the stem.

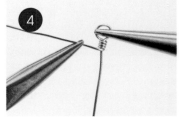

Grasp the loop with the chain-nose pliers. Use the second pair of chain-nose pliers to continue wrapping the wire around the stem 2–3 times more, moving from the loop downward.

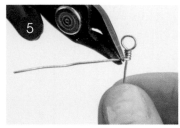

Use wire cutters to trim away any excess wire. Use emery cloth to smooth the rough wire end.

Use the chain-nose pliers to squeeze the cut end of the wire flush against the stem.

To make a second wrapped-wire loop at the opposite side of the bead, repeat steps 2–6.

HOW TO MAKE A SINGLE- AND A DOUBLE-OVERHAND KNOT

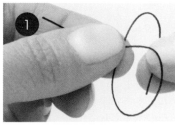

Cross the right thread over the left. Bring it around the back and through the center of the loop.

Pull the ends of the thread to make a single-overhand knot.

To make a double-overhand knot, repeat steps 1–2.

Then pull the ends of the threads to secure the knot in place.

HOW TO CONNECT WRAPPED-WIRE LOOPS TO MAKE A CHAIN

Prepare a bead with a wrapped-wire loop at each end; set the bead unit aside. Make a wrapped-wire loop on one end of a 6-in. (15.2cm) length of wire, and thread on one bead.

Rotate the bead so that it rests on the wrapped-wire loop. Grasp the straight wire ⅛ in. (3.0mm) above the bead using the chain-nose pliers. Turn the pliers away from you to bend the wire at a 90-deg. angle.

Grasp the wire ⅛ in. (3.0mm) from the bend using the round-nose pliers. Rotate the pliers toward the bend, and use your fingers to bend the wire around the jaw of the pliers. Cross the wire in front of the stem to make a loop, leaving a narrow gap.

DETAIL: The loop should have a narrow gap through which a wrapped-wire loop from another bead unit can pass.

Insert the wire that extends from the bead (worked in step 3) through one wrapped-wire loop on the bead unit (set aside in step 1), sliding the bead unit along the wire until the two beads are connected at their loops. Use the wire that extends from the bead to complete the wrapped-wire loop, moving the bead unit aside to do so.

To add another bead, make a wrapped-wire loop on one end of a 6-in. (15.2cm) length of wire, and thread on one bead. Then repeat steps 2–4. Continue to add as many bead units as desired to make a beaded chain of any length.

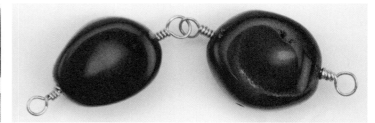

Two coral bead units connected by their wrapped-wire loops should look like this.

TIPS FOR USING ROUND-NOSE PLIERS: Round-nose pliers have a unique design that allows them to be used to create wire loops of different sizes, either very small or very large, depending upon where on the jaws of the pliers the wire is placed. When a wire is wrapped around the tips of the pliers, the resulting loop is small. When the wire is placed farther back on the jaws of the pliers (toward the joint) where the width increases, the loops are larger. To make loops that are consistent in size, mark a point on the pliers' jaws with a pencil, placing the wire on that spot each time you make a loop.

HOW TO MAKE AN EYE LOOP

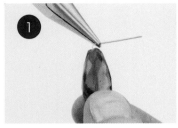

Insert a headpin through a bead. Use chain-nose pliers to grasp the headpin directly above the bead. Turn the pliers away from you to bend the stem at a 90-deg. angle.

Use round-nose pliers to grasp the stem 1/8 in. (3.0mm) from the bend, rotating the pliers toward the bend. Use your fingers to wrap the wire around one jaw of the pliers, crossing the wire in front to make a loop.

Use wire cutters to cut the wire where the end of the loop meets the stem. Use emery cloth to smooth the rough wire end.

DETAIL: The eye loop should look like this.

HOW TO MAKE AN EYE LOOP AT BOTH ENDS

Use wire cutters to cut a 6-in. (15.2cm) length of wire. Use chain-nose pliers to grasp the wire 1 in. (2.5cm) from the end. Turn the pliers away from you to bend the wire at a 90-deg. angle.

Use the round-nose pliers to grasp the wire 1/8 in. (3.0mm) from the bend. Rotate the pliers toward the bend.

Use your fingers to bend the wire around one jaw of the pliers, crossing the wire in front to make a loop.

Use wire cutters to cut the wire where the end of the loop meets the stem. Use emery cloth to smooth the rough wire end.

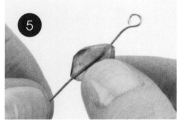

Thread a bead onto the wire.

Rotate the wire so that the bead sits on the eye loop. Use chain-nose pliers to grasp the wire directly above the bead. Turn the pliers away from you to bend the headpin at a 90-deg. angle.

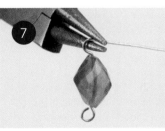

Use the round-nose pliers to grasp the wire 1/8 in. (3.0mm) from the bend. Rotate the pliers toward the bend.

Bend the wire around the jaw of the pliers, and cross it in front to make a loop. Use wire cutters to cut the wire where the end of the loop meets the stem. Use emery cloth to smooth the rough wire end.

HOW TO OPEN AND CLOSE AN EYE LOOP

To open the loop, grasp the cut end of the wire loop, and rotate it toward you using the chain-nose pliers, making a gap.

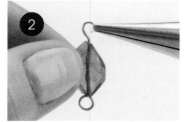

To close the loop, use the chain-nose pliers to grasp the cut end of the wire, and rotate it away from you until the cut end touches the stem.

HOW TO MAKE A BEADED FLOWER

Cut a 10-in. (25.4cm) length of wire. Insert one end of the wire into one briolette, and slide it to the wire's midpoint. Thread on another briolette. Gently bend the wire so that adjacent beads are touching.

Continue to add briolettes one-at-a-time, bending the wire as in step 1, until all the beads are threaded. Then cross the wires as shown.

Twist the wires together three times as shown, easing the briolettes on the wire to form a five-petal "flower."

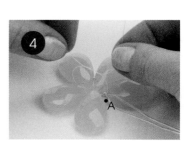

Cut a 12-in. (30.5cm) length of transite. Lay the flower on the transite, wrong side up, so that approx. 4 in. (10.1cm) extends to one side and 8 in. (20.3cm) extends to the other side. Bring the ends of transite around to A, and tie two double-overhand knots.

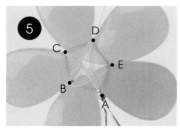

To secure the beads and to keep them from swiveling on the wire, bring the longer length of transite from A across the flower, and thread it between two beads at D; bring the transite underneath the flower and back up between two beads at B. Bring the transite back across the flower, and thread it between two beads at E; bring the transite underneath the flower and back up between two beads at C. Bring the transite back across the flower, and thread it between two beads at A; bring the transite underneath the flower and back up between two beads at D. Continue the winding pattern, going around the flower two more times. Tie two double-overhand knots using the short length of transite set aside in step 4 to secure the transite. Note: Do not cut the transite.

Turn the flower right side up. Bring the longer length of transite around to the top, and thread on one round bead. Slide the bead down, centering it in the briolettes. Bring the transite underneath the flower, and use the second length of transite to tie several knots. Trim away the excess transite.

To make the wire loop, use wire cutters to cut the wire stems affixed in steps 1–3 to 1 in. (2.5cm). Use the round-nose pliers to grasp the ends of the wires, and rotate them toward the center of the flower, creating a coil-shape loop. Note: this loop is used with a jump ring to secure the flower to a link in a bracelet.

HOW TO MAKE THE BEADED "WILD ORCHID" BOUQUET

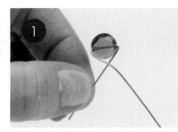

PURPLE FLOWER: Use wire cutters to cut a 10-in. (25.4cm) length of gold wire. Thread on one aubergine disc 1 in. (2.5cm) from one end. Bend both ends of wire around the bead, and cross the ends as shown.

Twist the wires together, using chain-nose pliers to secure the twist, if necessary.
Note: there will be one short and one long wire.

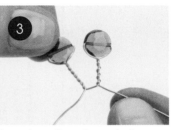

Thread another disc onto the long wire, positioning the disc 1 in. (2.5cm) from the end of the twist. Repeat step 2.

Continue to add beads to the long wire until there is no wire left. Repeat steps 1–4 to make more beaded strands until all the beads are used. Gather and twist the beaded strands together to make a "flower."

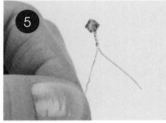

BLUE FLORAL SPRAY: Use wire cutters to cut a 6-in. (15.2cm) length of gold wire. Thread on one blue bicone 1½ in. (3.8cm) from one end. Bend both ends of wire around the bead, and cross them. Twist the wires together until the twisted stem measures ¼-in. (6.0mm) long.

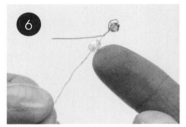

Bend the short wire to one side. Thread a light-blue round bead onto the long wire, and slide it along the wire, stopping at the twist.

Bring the short wire along the outside of the light-blue bead, and twist it together with the long wire to secure the bead. Set the floral stem aside. Repeat the steps to make six more floral stems as before.

Gather and twist the floral stems together to make a blue floral spray.

GREEN-LEAF CLUSTER: Use wire cutters to cut two 6-in. (15.2cm) lengths of gold wire. Set one wire aside. Thread on one green oval, one new-jade rondelle, and one green oval. Position the beads at the midpoint of the wire. Bend both wires down as shown.

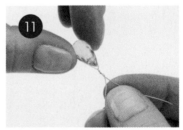

Cross the wires under the green ovals, positioning the rondelle at the top. Twist the wires together to make one green-leaf cluster. Repeat to make the second green-leaf cluster.

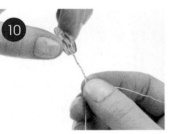

YELLOW-BRIOLETTE CLUSTER (AND THE VARIEGATED PINK BUD (not shown)): Cut three 6-in. (15.2cm) lengths of gold wire. Set two aside. Center one briolette on the wire, and twist the wires to form a stem.

Repeat step 11 to make two more twisted-wire briolettes. Gather and twist the wired briolettes together to make a cluster. Repeat step 11 to make one pink bud using the variegated-pink bead.

index of techniques and applications

necklace and bracelet lengths

NECKLACE
Choker: 16 in. (40.6cm)
Princess: 18–20 in. (40.5cm–50.8cm)
Matinee: 23–27 in. (58.4cm–68.6cm)
Opera: 35–37 in. (88.9cm–94.0cm)

BRACELET
Women's: 7 in. (17.8cm)
Men's: 9 in. (22.9cm)
Anklet: 10 in. (25.4cm)

chart of measurements

Beads are commonly measured in millimeters (mm). Generally, the higher the number, the larger the bead.
The exception to this is seed beads, whose size is indicated by numbers. The higher the number, the smaller the bead.
A size 5° seed bead is about 5mm wide; a size 11 is about 2mm wide.

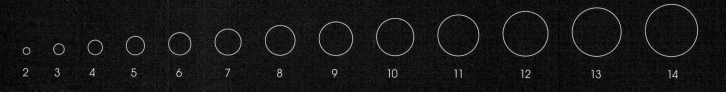

2 3 4 5 6 7 8 9 10 11 12 13 14

Sources and Resources

BAZAAR STAR BEADERY
216 East Ridgewood Ave.
Ridgewood, NJ 07450
201.444.5144
www.bazaarstarbeadery.com
Loose and strung beads

BLUE MOON BEADS®
7855 Hayvenhurst Ave.
Van Nuys, CA 91406
800.377.6715
www.bluemoonbeads.com
Beads and findings

FIRE MOUNTAIN GEMS AND BEADS
One Fire Mountain Way
Grants Pass, OR 97526
800.423.2319
www.firemountaingems.com
Beads and findings

FUN 2 BEAD
1028 Sixth Ave.
New York, NY 10018
212.302.3488 www.fun2bead.com
Loose and strung beads, findings

GENUINE TEN TEN
1010 Sixth Ave.
New York, NY 10018
212.221.1173
Loose and strung beads, findings

M&J TRIMMING
1008 Sixth Ave., New York, NY 10018
212.204.9595
800.965.8746 www.mjtrim.com
Ribbons and beads

MICHAELS STORES, INC.
8000 Bent Branch Dr.
Irving, TX 75063
800.642.4235 www.michaels.com
National craft supply store with
comprehensive beading section

NEW YORK BEADS
1026 Sixth Ave.
New York, NY 10018
212.382.2994
Loose and strung beads

TINSEL TRADING
47 West 38th St.
New York, NY 10018
212.730.1030 www.tinseltrading.com
Beads, cords, and ribbons

TOHO SHOJI
990 Sixth Ave.
New York, NY 10018
212.868.7466 www.tohoshojiny.com
Beads, findings, chains, and charms

TRIM WORLD USA
49 West 37th St.
New York, NY 10018
212.391.1046 www.trim-world.co.kr
Loose and strung beads, and gold and
silver findings

Acknowledgments

I would like to thank the entire team at Creative Homeowner for all their hard work, particularly my mother for her love and unparalleled dedication, and Tim Bakke for his support of this project. Thanks also to Jennifer Calvert and Nora Grace for their great efforts and good cheer; and a special thanks to Frank Dyer and Kim Vivas in production.

Thank you to my incredibly talented team: Damian Sandone, for his kindness and never-ending generosity; Steven Mays, for his friendship and ability to endure long, long days with great humor; Robin Delpino, who saved the day with incredible grace and intelligence; Anne Newgarden, for her unique ability to turn a colorful phrase; and Frank Santopadre, for keeping me on deadline, fed, and sane.

Thank you to Diane Shaw and Kathryn Hammill at Goodesign for their beautiful work. And thank you to Candie Frankel for her editing expertise.

And finally, a special thanks to Iliana McGrath and Blue Moon Beads for their generous contribution of the most spectacular beads and findings.

Index